D1522341

the Family Bible Study Book

the Family Bible Study Book

Betsey Scanlan, Editor

Fleming H. Revell Company
Old Tappan, New Jersey

Library of Congress Cataloging in Publication Data

Main entry under title:

The Family Bible study book.

Bibliography: p.
Includes indexes.
1. Bible—Study—Text-books. I. Scanlan, Betsey.
BS605.2.F35 220′.07 75-5680
ISBN 0-8007-0730-3

Printed in the United States of America

CONTENTS

For all Scripture is inspired by God and useful for teaching the truth, rebuking error, correcting faults, and giving instructions for right living, so that the man who serves God may be fully qualified and equipped to do every kind of good work.

2 Timothy 3:16, 17 TEV

INTRODUCTION

THE WHY OF *THE FAMILY BIBLE STUDY BOOK*

Walk into any Christian bookstore: look at a catalog from just about any religious publishing house, and you'll see literally hundreds of Bible study guides. Sunday-school teachers, neighborhood Bible study groups and couples' clubs wishing to study the Scriptures have much excellent material from which to choose.

So why THIS Bible study book? Because it's been carefully planned and created for *family* study! The lessons are designed for the use of entire families from the youngest child to the senior citizen who may live at your house. It was the unanimous opinion of the thirteen authors of *The Family Bible Study Book* that this was the great single need today in Bible study: a book that the entire family could use in discovering the Scriptures—one so flexible that it could be used in any family, regardless of its size and the ages of its members. Because there are thirteen authors, there is a wide variety of format.

Who are the authors? The complete list, with brief biographies, may be found in the back of the book. Although differing in education, professional, cultural, denominational, and geographic origin, they have three things in common: all are Christians, all are mothers, and all have been involved in Bible study and/or Sunday-school teaching. *And* they all agreed that they had found no one book suitable for family use in Scripture study.

How were the books selected for this study? This was one of the hardest decisions to make. It was determined that a verse by verse study would be almost impossible if more than one or two books were to be covered. It was decided to highlight five books, although the readers will find the studies for most books pretty comprehensive. Genesis and Acts were very nearly unanimous choices. John was the popular selection for the Gospels, and Ephesians the choice of Paul's letters. Proverbs and Psalms were so close another vote had to be taken before Proverbs was selected. Each of the authors was assigned lessons in three different books, with certain chapters to be covered in each. The only specific instructions were that each lesson was to be approximately fifteen minutes in length, that each lesson should open with a prayer asking God's wisdom and guidance in understanding the Scriptures, and close with a prayer. Also, that exposition was to be kept to a minimum, although a brief summary setting the scene was acceptable. Each author was asked to submit general suggestions for family Bible study, and a brief background summary of one of the books of the Bible included in this volume. (That is, the summary would include the time it was written and by whom—if known; the attending circumstances, and its importance in the overall Scripture picture.) Each writer prepared her own format and every lesson was family-tested, often by more than one family.

GENERAL SUGGESTIONS FOR FAMILY BIBLE STUDY

It's almost impossible to give all the wonderful suggestions submitted by the thirteen authors, but here are some general points of agreement.

Regular time for the lessons should be set if possible. Most agreed that after dinner (before dessert?) was the best time. Again, this will differ from family to family. If there is no time when everyone is present every day, then schedule it either for several times each week or proceed whether or not everyone is present. Maybe Daddy works shift work or travels a good deal. As children grow up and have jobs of their own, don't cancel out because someone is missing. Keep the project afloat even if only one parent is present. Once a week is better than not at all; doing it with one or more members absent is better than not doing it at all! And remember, never wait for an ideal time.

The attitude of the parent toward the lessons is important. The parents should enter into the Bible study with an attitude of joy rather than duty. The Scriptures *are* exciting and should be presented that way. But it's important, too, that the children feel that this is a *family* program, not just for them.

Let's all participate. Everyone should be encouraged to join in but should not be forced to answer the questions or be "put on the spot." Don't let one member dominate the discussion—but at the same time, if someone chooses not to participate, avoid embarrassing or making an example of him. And above all, *don't* choose this time to lecture or discipline. It should be used to build up and encourage one another. Provide a quiet amusement (crayons or puzzles) for the smallest fry during the lessons. Perhaps a special activity book could be reserved just for this time. Some lessons lend themselves to drawing—Noah's Ark, for instance. If the younger children can't participate, they should be part of the family circle during the family Bible study time. And don't hesitate to include guests. In this way, family Bible study can also be a means of evangelism.

What Bible to use? All of the authors agreed that one of the modern versions (Good News for Modern Man, The Living Bible) is easier for children to follow. It isn't necessary for all to have the same version (the adults might prefer their King James or Revised Standard) but the one conducting the lesson should use a simplified version if there are young children in the family. If each member has his own Bible, he can have the Bible open to the passage under discussion. This does make it easier to answer the questions.

Other suggestions for your family's consideration are included.

PRAYER: Family members should be encouraged to make requests either at the opening or closing of the lesson, A list might be kept for review each time the family prays together. Be sure to thank God for answering before crossing off an answered prayer request. You can try short prayers all around or the leader might pray for all requests. Some of the lessons suggest prayers to be said, but families are encouraged to express personal prayers.

YOUNGER CHILDREN: Every effort should be made to include the younger children, but neither you nor they should become discouraged if they don't have a total grasp of the Scripture being studied. If they learn one truth in each lesson consider it a success. Although many of the lessons have questions directed to various age groups, some contain both simple and more complicated queries. It is up to the father (or whoever is leading the lesson) to determine which questions are more suitable for young children and direct them accordingly. Younger children will be fidgety and you should expect it. But like any form of study, Bible study *is* a discipline: it is an act of obedience to come together to study God's Word and He will honor it.

SINGING: Some families just love to sing. Others consider themselves tone deaf. If your clan is composed of singers, join together in praising the Lord in song with or without the piano, organ, or other musical instruments. If you don't sing, then read an appropriate hymn. Let the younger children select the hymns if possible.

DRAMA: Role-playing is "in" now and some families really enjoy dramatic portrayal of the Scriptures. It's a fine opportunity for children to become a part of the action, and chances are the Bible story will be remembered for a long, long time. (Better do this *after* prayer time.)

DISCUSSION QUESTIONS: They do help bring out the meaning of the Scripture and help insure that everyone has grasped what has been read. Teens particularly enjoy such discussions. Also it is a good time for personal application. (How does this apply to me? What does this mean to me personally?)

HOW TO USE *THE FAMILY BIBLE STUDY BOOK*

How long should the lesson be?

The lessons are designed for approximately fifteen minutes each, but family discussions, dramas, or singing may mean a longer period of time is spent. It's up to the individual families how long the lesson should be. Some families may decide to stop in the middle of an especially difficult lesson and complete it the next evening. Some—especially if there are older children—may want to go on to the next lesson. There is a great flexibility—or should be. Some items are marked "optional" or "for further discussion." If you want to continue the study for a longer period utilize these suggestions. Nor is it necessary to start with Genesis. Some families may prefer to go right into the New Testament or start with Proverbs. It's *your* family and *your* Family Bible Study Book!

Use the comprehensive index. Suppose you are looking for a lesson on a specific theme (*truth, love, purity, honesty*) or biblical personality (Joseph, Ananias, Stephen). Instead of following the studies in chronological order, you'll find the lessons concerned with a specific topic under *Themes* or *Topics* or the name of the person. (This is still another way to provide variety in your family's study of God's Word.)

WHY the wide margins? These are for jotting down comments about the lessons, what family members said, suggestions for further study, prayer requests. Chances are, unless you are an exceptional Bible scholar, there will be questions you cannot answer. Don't be disturbed by this. Indicate so in the margin of that lesson and go back to it later.

Notice the special lessons for teens. There are lessons specified for teen-agers. You can find them so designated in the text (and in the index). If they don't apply to your family, go on to the next lesson.

For further study or more background material, use the bibliography just before the index. Perhaps your appetite will be whetted during these lessons, so we've listed some helpful books you may want to secure at your local bookstore or church library. The Song Index will help you locate suitable hymns that are suggested in some of the lessons.

TELL US WHAT YOU THINK OF *THE FAMILY BIBLE STUDY BOOK*

After your family has used this book, we would like to know what you think of it. Fill out the evaluation sheet on the inside back flap of the book jacket. Detach and mail to us. Your suggestions will be taken into prayerful and careful consideration in the preparation of any future study books.

> For where two or three are gathered together in my name, there am I in the midst of them.
>
> Matthew 18:20

Christ is ready to join your family. It is our sincere hope that these studies will encourage your family to welcome Him.

THE PUBLISHERS

Light and Dark Day and Night
Day 1
Day 2
Water Heavens Water
Land (earth) Seas Vegetation Trees
Day 3
Day 4
Sun Moon Stars
Fish, Water Creatures Birds
Day 5
Day 6
Domestic and Wild Animals Creeping Things Mankind
God Rested
Day 7

Studies in Genesis

The Book of Genesis gives us important (essential!) foundation stones for our Christian faith. Genesis is, indeed, a book of beginnings: the beginning of the world, man, sin, the family; also the beginning of nations and languages. All of the topics touched upon in Genesis are further discussed and expounded upon throughout the rest of the Bible.

In this book, God sets in motion His great plan for reclaiming His own creatures who had disobeyed Him and foreshadows the need for a Saviour to redeem man from sin. Chapters 1–11 discuss Creation and the human race in general with specific accounts of Adam and Eve and Noah and his family. The remaining chapters deal with the beginning of the Hebrew race by its founding through Abraham, and then the development and history of the Hebrews through Isaac, Jacob, and Joseph (a total period of about two thousand years). The lives of these ancients and patriarchs are highly interesting, but they are secondary to the Presence and activity of God, the Supreme Character in this great drama.

Throughout Genesis, we see God in His eternal existence, His power and wisdom, His righteous judgment, His enduring patience, mercy, and forgiveness—and His infinite love for mankind. In Genesis, we find this love beginning with His covenant promise and reaching through all of Scripture to touch us in our own day in the Person of Jesus Christ.

It is both the traditional Hebrew and Christian position that Moses, inspired by the Spirit of God, wrote the Book of Genesis from ancient documents. (He also wrote the four books that follow.)

God called on the people of Israel to teach their children about the mighty works of God (*see* Joshua 4:21–24). In ancient days, the knowledge of the Almighty was passed from father to son and so it can be taught in families today. As you begin the "Book of Beginnings," may it be a beginning of a greater appreciation and knowledge of God's Word in your own family.

(NOTE: Some lessons are marked *A* for "alternate." These present a different aspect of the same passages. For greater understanding, you may want to do both lessons. At the end of the section, there are some Open-Book Quizzes to sharpen your knowledge of this Book of Beginnings. A Creation Worship Service concludes this section.

Genesis particularly lends itself to drawings and clay work for the younger children. While the older members of the family are studying the lessons, the small fry can draw or paint the Garden of Eden, the animals, and plants. They can make other scenes from Genesis with construction-paper tents and palm trees, and pipecleaner or clay animals. Use your imagination and the materials around the house!)

BEGINNING OF BEGINNINGS—GENESIS 1:1–10

1

Opening Prayer

We praise You, Lord, that You are stronger than Satan who tries to destroy truth. As we start to study Your Word, send the Holy Spirit to open our understanding and increase our faith. We pray in the name of our Saviour Jesus Christ. *Amen.*

Scripture Reading

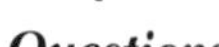

Questions

Genesis 1:1, 2

AGES 3–8 A Who was in the beginning? What did He create?

AGES 9–14 B What kind of picture does "without form and empty waste and darkness" bring to your mind?

ADULT C What part of the Triune God is specifically mentioned here and what is He doing?

Genesis 1:3–5

A What was created first?

B How did God create light? What was light called? What was darkness called?

C Light is a very prominent word in all the Scriptures. Jesus Christ is called "a light into the world" (John 12:46).

Briefly give the results of light in general. (For outside consideration read John 1:4, 5 and John 12:35–50.)

Genesis 1:6–8

- A What was created on the second day? Who made it happen?
- B When God speaks, does what He says always happen?
- C Time is being measured by one day being one period of light and one period of darkness. Does this limit this day to the same length of time as our present day (2 Peter 3:8)?

Genesis 1:9, 10

- A Was God pleased with the land and the sea that He had just made? When you see beautiful mountains and the ocean, do you remember who made them?
- B Who named the land and the waters and what did He call them?
- C What expressions in verses 3, 7 and 9 emphasize the results when God speaks? Does God change?

Conclusion

Read Romans 1:19–23 (preferably a modern version). If there is time, sing a verse of the hymn "How Great Thou Art."

Closing Prayer

Dear Father, Your greatness is far beyond our human comprehension! We thank You for the privilege of learning Your truths. Help us to live as Your children. *Amen.*

(Reference Material: *Man Does Not Stand Alone* by A. Cressy Morrison; *Seven Reasons Why a Scientist Believes in God* by A. Cressy Morrison; *Your God Is Too Small* by J. B. Phillips.)

BEGINNING OF BEGINNINGS—GENESIS 1:11–25 (Continued)

2

Opening Prayer

Praise that God is God and not a figment of man's imagination.

Scripture Reading

Questions

Genesis 1:11–13

- A What day did God make the grass, plants, and trees? (Show Creation Chart.)
- B What else has been made on this same day? (Show Creation Chart.)
- C What reference is made to reproduction? Is there room for

evolution here? What is God's response as He views what has been created these first three days?

Genesis 1:14–19

A What lights do you see in the sky in the daytime? In the night? Who made them?

B Try to find four reasons God gave these lights.

C What do you see in this passage that shows God's concern and intricate design for things He has created?

Genesis 1:20–23

A What did God create in the waters? What in the air?

B What does verse 21 say that birds (fowls) had in the very beginning?

C Explain what "according to their kinds," or "after his kind" indicates. What is God's attitude and command to these first living creatures?

Genesis 1:24, 25 (NOTE: The Amplified Bible uses "wild beasts" for "beasts of the earth" and "domestic animals" for "cattle.")

A What was the only thing God had to do to have animals on the earth?

B Does God want the animals to interbreed and have babies?

C Underline on chart the things God has created up to the end of verse 25. God's pleasure in His Creation is expressed by how frequently the expression "it was good" is repeated. How do we view and treat these same creations?

Discussion (optional)

We say an artist creates a masterpiece or an architect creates a very different kind of building. Why was God's creative work absolutely unlike any man's (*see* Hebrews 11:3)?

Conclusion

The hymn "It Took a Miracle" by John Peterson.

My Father is omnipotent, and that you can't deny
A God of might and miracles. 'Tis written in the sky.
It took a miracle to hang the world in space
It took a miracle to put the stars in place
But when He saved my soul
Cleaned and made me whole
It took a miracle of love and grace.

Closing Prayer

Lord, we praise You for this beautiful world that You have created. Thank You for wanting us in Your image and providing for all our needs. Help us to love You with all our hearts. In Jesus' Name, we pray. *Amen.*

BEGINNING OF MAN—GENESIS 1:26–2:3

3

Prayer

Our Father who art in heaven hallowed be Thy name! We want to know about You and Your Kingdom. Put away human thoughts that would interfere with hearing Your truth. Thank You! In Jesus' Name. *Amen.*

Read Scripture

Questions

Genesis 1:26–28

A Who does God make like Himself? Over what does man have authority (rule, dominion)?

B What are the two different types of man that God created (v. 27)?
When man is mentioned in other verses of Scripture, does that include women?

C What plural pronoun shows the Trinity is present? What is God's command to man after He has blessed him? Since God created all things and then gave the command for man's actions, would man be equipped to do this?

Genesis 1:29–31

A Was God happy with everything He had made?

B What did God provide for man, animals, birds, and every living creature to eat?

C Go over the chart to see what was created each day. Quickly scan this chapter to see how often "It was so," "It was good," and "It was done" are stated. What do these statements emphasize about the results when God speaks? Does God's Word bring the same results in your life?

Genesis 2:1–3

A How many days did God work? What day did He rest?

B If we are created in the likeness of God and God rested on the seventh day, wouldn't this seem a good example for us? (*See* Mark 2:27; Romans 14:5, 6.)

C When God set the seventh day apart and hallowed it, whose day would it then be? What do you think would please God on the day set apart for Him? (Many of Jesus' experiences on the Jewish seventh day are recorded in the

New Testament and would be helpful in answering this question. *See* Matthew 12:1–13.)

Discussion (optional)

Verse 26 says God created man in His own image. In what way is man made in the likeness of God?

Conclusion

God created man (male and female) with the knowledge of all his needs; even the seventh day of rest was a gift from God.

Prayer

Lord, help me to see Your way is the best way. Help me to do the things that please You, not what please other men. Help me to seek Your truth and do it. *Amen.*

THE ROLE OF MEN AND WOMEN—GENESIS 1:26–31; 2:7–9, 18–25

4

Prayer

Pray that God will teach us what it means to be created in His image.

Read Scripture

Let's Talk About What We Have Read

How did God create man?

How is man different from everything else God made?

In Genesis 1:28, what task did God give man to do?

How can we carry out that task in the twentieth century?

Why did God make woman?

What task did God give her?

What are some ways a woman can be a helper to a man?

Because woman was created to be a helper to man, does that mean she is less of a person in God's sight?

How is the man/woman relationship fulfilled in marriage?

Let's Remember What We Have Read

1 God created man and woman in His image to be like Himself.

2 Man's responsibility is to care for what God has made. He is to live as a Christian in his relationship to the created world.

3 Woman was created to be a companion and helpmate for man. She is to join with him in the marriage relationship where God regards them as one.

Singing (optional)

Choose a song about God and the wonderful world He created (*see* Song Index).

Prayer

Let's thank God for His Creation. Each family member may wish to offer a sentence prayer of thanks for something he especially appreciates in God's Creation.

THE GARDEN OF EDEN—GENESIS 2:4–15

5

Prayer

Pray for an open mind while doing this study.

Read Scripture

Questions

Genesis 2:4–6

AGES 3–8 A What was there instead of rain when the earth was first formed?

AGES 9–14 B What hadn't sprung up as yet? (What are other words for herb or plant?)

ADULT C Who is needed in verse 5?

Genesis 2:7

A Who formed man?

B From what was man formed? (NOTE: From Amplified Bible —the same essential chemical elements are found in man and animal life that are found in the soil. This scientific fact was not known to man until recent times, but God was displaying it here.)

C After verse 4, there is an addition to the name of God. What does the name *Lord* mean to you? What does man receive that the other creations do not (1 Corinthians 15:45)?

Genesis 2:8, 9

A Where did the Lord God put man?

B How did the Lord God provide for man's physical need of food?

C What two trees are in the center of the Garden (Revelation 2:7; 22:14)?

Genesis 2:10–14

A Would you like gold, pearls, and jewels? Does a land that has many of these in it sound like a good place?

B How many riverheads are there?

C What do you think God is saying about Eden from these four verses?

Genesis 2:15

A Does a beautiful garden make you want to get out or stay in it?

B What does the Lord God tell man he should do in the Garden?

C Through these first chapters of Genesis, we see how the Lord God has provided for all His creations. Do you believe that this command to keep the Garden is a hardship?

Conclusion

God wants to supply our needs and the needs of His Creation.

Prayer

Sing or say "The Doxology."

(Reference material: *A Commentary on the Whole Bible,* vol. 1, Genesis–Deuteronomy by Matthew Henry.)

THE BEGINNING OF MARRIAGE— GENESIS 2:14–25

6

Prayer

Read Scripture

Questions

Genesis 2:16, 17

A Does this Scripture say that God says Adam cannot eat a certain apple?

B From how many trees can the man eat? From how many can't he eat? Does he have enough for all his needs?

C *Lord* and *command* are strong words. Do you believe Adam knew exactly what God said not to do? Do you think Adam knew what *to die* meant? Do you know what the meaning is in this passage?

Genesis 2:18

A Do you like to be all alone?

B Describe a helper.

C How is God's love shown in this verse?

Genesis 2:19, 20

A Who named all the living creatures?

B Can your favorite pet be a real helper to you?

C Can an animal ever completely take the place of a human companion? What limitations are there in animals?

Genesis 2:21, 22

A What part of Adam's body did God take to make Eve?

B What vital organ is under the rib cage? God never does anything "just for fun." (Can you think of a possible reason why the rib was the part of Adam from which Eve was formed?)

C Who brings the woman to Adam? Discuss what this means to a Christian husband and wife.

Genesis 2:23–25

A Do you purposely hurt any part of your body?

B Who should the man leave to take a wife?

C Do husbands and wives often try to hide things (thoughts) from one another? If you are united by God and truly one flesh, how will this be expressed in your actions and reactions to each other?

Conclusion

God's plan of Creation centered around man in His image. God's love and concern were shown by all the provisions He made for man's welfare and happiness, but man was still a free agent to obey or disobey. This option is still in force today.

Discussion

God made man a free moral agent and gave him the choice of obedience or disobedience. Which choice do we as a family and as individuals make during our daily routines? At work? At school? At play?

Prayer

Pray specifically about decisions the family or a member of the family may be faced with at this time.

THE FALL OF MAN—GENESIS 2:15–17; 3:1–24

7

Prayer

Our Father and Creator, we ask that Your Holy Spirit will touch us deeply with the Scripture we read today. Only after realizing the fact of our sin can we come to know You through the sacrificial death of Your Son, Jesus Christ. *Amen.*

Let's Read God's Word

Genesis 2:15–17, 3:1–24

Let's Talk About What We Have Read

What was the one rule God made that Adam and Eve must obey?

Why did the serpent come to Eve first?

How did he get her to talk about the matter with him?

How did he try to make her stop having faith in God?

Was Adam functioning as the leader in his relationship with Eve?

What change took place in Adam and Eve once they ate the fruit?

How do you think Adam and Eve felt when they heard God's footsteps in the Garden after they sinned? How do you think they felt before they sinned?

What was the attitude of Adam and Eve when God confronted them with their disobedience?

Were Adam and Eve and the serpent punished for disobeying God's law? How?

Let's Remember

1 God is the Source of law and justice.
2 Adam and Eve disobeyed God's law and were punished. This changed the relationship of God and man even to the present day.
3 Although God knew Adam and Eve had sinned, He still sought them in the Garden as He seeks us today.

Prayer

Let's thank God that, though we are all heir to Adam and Eve's original sin, we can be restored to fellowship with Him through believing in the Lord Jesus Christ whose death paid the penalty for sin. *Amen.*

(NOTE TO PARENTS: Further discussion of this lesson is encouraged in the hope that God will use it in your family to bring each of the members into a saving relationship with Him.)

THE FALL OF MAN—GENESIS 2:15–17; 3:1–7

7A

Prayer

Read Scripture

Questions

Genesis 1:31

How did God feel about man, and everything else He had just created?

Genesis 6:5–7

1 Five chapters later: now how does God feel about the man he made?

2 What caused the change?

To see what brought about this tragic change in God's Creation, read Genesis 2:15–17; 3:1–7.

1 In the beautiful Garden of Eden there was only one thing God said man was not to do. What was it?
2 Who first put the idea of disobedience into the woman?
3 Did this act of disobedience seem like an evil thing to the woman? How did it seem to her?
4 Can you think of any disobedience of yours that at the time seemed like a good thing?
5 What effect does Adam's disobedience have upon you? (*See* Romans 5:19.)

Conclusion

In Romans 6:23, you'll find God's great remedy for human sin —yours and mine.

Food for Thought (optional)

A In Romans 14:12 RSV, we read, "So each of us shall give account of himself to God." Before God, do we take full responsibility for our own actions? Can we blame others for our own acts?

B Romans 3:23 RSV states, ". . . all have sinned and fall short of the glory of God. . . ." Ever since Adam and Eve, sin has been a problem for mankind. Exactly how has God provided an answer to this sin problem?

Prayer

Ask the Lord to reveal the areas of sin in our own lives so that we may confess our sins.

CAIN DISOBEYS GOD—GENESIS 4:16, 25, 26

8

Prayer

Pray that God will teach us from His Word the lessons we can learn from the story of Cain and Abel.

Introduction

Adam and Eve were driven outside the Garden by the Lord God and told to till the ground. Because they knew they were naked, God had clothed them with skins which is the first indication of the shedding of blood because of the sin of man.

Let's Read God's Word

Genesis 4:1–16, 25, 26 (optional Hebrews 11:14 LB)

Let's Talk About What We Have Read

What did Cain and Abel do for a living?

What gifts did they bring to the Lord at harvest time?

How did Cain respond to God's rejection of his offering?

Did this show that he had faith in God?

After Cain disobeyed God, how did he act?

When God saw that Cain was angry and rebellious, what warning did He give him?

How did God punish Cain for his sin?

In what way did God show Cain mercy even in his punishment?

Let's Remember

1 A sacrifice to God made with an obedient heart in the way that God requires is the only kind He accepts.
2 Cain did not bring the first fruits to God. His rebellion led to great sin.
3 God did not fail to punish Cain.

Prayer

Encourage each one around the table to ask God to give him an obedient heart.

DESTRUCTION AND NEW BEGINNING— GENESIS 6–8

9

Prayer

Open with a prayer of thanks for this portion of Scripture and ask for an open heart and mind to understand the meaning of this chapter.

Introduction

Many, many centuries have passed and descendants of Adam and Eve have populated the earth. Evil and sin have become so rampant that the Lord has no fellowship with man—the reason man was created—and therefore is going to destroy man, beast, and creeping things and fowls of the air.

Read

Genesis 6:8, 9, 14, 17–22; 7:10, 23; 8:14–17

Questions

Genesis 6:8, 9

AGES 3–8 A Was Noah a good man? When you walk with someone, are you usually fighting or having a good time together?

AGES 9–13 B How does God feel about Noah? Why?

ADULT C Does this passage say Noah was without sin? What then seems to be the reason he found favor with God?

Genesis 6:14, 17–22 (Have younger children draw a picture of the Ark.)

A What did God tell Noah to build? Why? Did Noah do it?

B What is God's punishment for the evil on the earth at that time? Who is not to receive this punishment?

C What is a covenant? What is needed to make a covenant binding?

Genesis 7:10, 23

A Did God do what He said He would?

B What people are still alive?

C Will Noah and his family always be alive? For what purpose were they saved at this time?

Conclusion

God cannot let evil continue indefinitely, but, with compassion, makes a way to escape, if we are willing to obey and accept His plan for salvation.

Food for Thought (optional)

Try to imagine and discuss what the people must have thought about Noah building the Ark and of all his probable warnings to the people.

(A cubit is the length between the elbows and fingertip. Figuring an average of 18 inches, one estimates the Ark to be 450 feet long, 75 feet wide, and 45 feet high.)

Prayer

Dear Lord, make all of us more like Noah—people full of faith who are a pleasure to You. *Amen.*

THE FLOOD—GENESIS 8–9:1–17

(The Revised Standard Version is used in this lesson.)

10

Prayer

Open the lesson with a prayer for the many, many blessings of the day and the opportunity to study God's Word. Help us to understand God's great power and the control that He has over the earth. Also ask for an open mind to understand these chapters.

Read Scripture

Genesis 8

Questions

1 Where did the Ark come to rest when the flood waters receded?

2 How long was it until Noah and the other inhabitants could leave the Ark? (You may need pencil and paper for this.)

3 After leaving the Ark, what was one of the first things that Noah did?

4 What promises did the Lord give to us in these verses?

Read Scripture

Genesis 9:1–17

5 Was God eager to populate the earth again? What did He tell Noah and his sons?

6 What was man's only restriction regarding the food he should eat?

7 What was the punishment for murder in these times?

8 What was God's covenant with Noah?

9 What is the sign of this covenant?

10 What do we know God is doing when we see a rainbow in the sky? Genesis 9:28, 29 states, "After the flood Noah lived three hundred and fifty years. All the days of Noah were nine hundred and fifty years; and he died."

Food for Thought (optional)

During the flood, God cared for Noah in great detail. Contemplate and discuss the many ways in which God has cared and provided for us. Think of nature in all of its detail and how we benefit. Also think of all the systems of your body and how they work together.

Prayer

Close with prayer, being thankful for this portion of Scripture and His great love for us.

THE TOWER OF BABEL—GENESIS 11:1–9

(The Revised Standard Version is used in this study.)

11

Prayer

Open the lesson with prayer, having each member of the family contribute his thanks and possible requests. Pray especially for an understanding of this portion of Scripture.

Introduction

Genesis 10 tells of the genealogies of Noah's sons. At the end of the genealogy for each son, there is a verse stating that each son and his descendants have their own language and their own nation. Genesis 11 gives us an account of how the dispersion (or separation) of people came about. (Younger children may want to draw a picture of the tower.)

Read Scripture

Genesis 11:1–9

Questions

1 How many languages were used on the whole earth?
2 What does the word *migrate* mean? Probably a high percentage of Noah's sons and their families were nomadic. In Genesis 8:16, 17 and 9:7, God commands the people to take all the animals from the Ark so that they can multiply on the earth. Men were to do the same.
3 What did the people do when they reached Shinar? Did this seem to be God's will, if verses 8:16, 17 and 9:7 were followed?
4 Now, what are they planning to do? Why? Are they following God's plan for them?
5 What does this verse show us about the Lord in relation to His people?
6 What was the Lord's evaluation of the situation?
7 When the Lord said, "Let us go down . . ." to whom does the word *us* refer?
8 Exactly what did the Lord do to these people? Does this seem cruel? Remember that the Lord had made His plans known to them through Noah. This land was known to be fertile, and you can understand how they may have wanted to stay in one place with city walls as protection. Yet, if they had the faith of Noah, they would not have had to worry about protection or food for their flocks. Man so often feels self-sufficient and lacks the knowledge of his need of God.
9 What did the Lord do to fulfill His plan to populate the whole earth?
10 What name was given to that area where the city and tower were being built?

Conclusion

These were a proud people who wanted to make a name for themselves. There have been towers excavated in that area which seem to have been used in pagan worship. The tower mentioned in these verses could have been such a tower. In the Bible, this city increasingly came to symbolize the godless society. (*See* Isaiah 47:8–13.)

Food for Thought

Do we know the teachings of the Bible and then often do otherwise? Think of some examples of this in your own life.

Prayer

Close with a prayer of thanksgiving and a request for being led and guided in the direction that would be pleasing to the Lord.

(Suggested Reading: *Genesis, an Introduction and Commentary* by Derek Kidner.)

GENESIS 12:1–9

12

Prayer

Introduction

Someone has said that Chapter 12 is the "dividing point" of the Bible. God's good Creation was infected with sin. What can be done about it? From Genesis 12:1, God says, "I'll show you what can be done about it."

A man : a family : a nation : the Saviour.

Read Scripture

Questions

1 Of all the people living at that time whom does God call? What does He ask him to do?
2 What promise does God make to Abram? Does God always fulfill His promises?
3 God promised that all the families of the earth would be blessed by Abram. To whom is this pointing?
4 How did Abram respond to this Word from God?
5 On this long walk from his home to Canaan (about 1,100 miles), who went with Abram?
6 What was the first thing Abram did when he got to the new, strange land?
7 God does not speak directly to us as He did to Abram. How does He let us know what He wants us to do? Let each member of the family share one specific area in which he will try to obey God this week.

Prayer

Close with a prayer of thanksgiving for the opportunity to read and study the Bible. Ask that God may make each of us aware of our great need of Him and His Word.

BEGINNING OF THE SPECIAL RACE— GENESIS 12:1–8

12A

Prayer

Introduction

Noah's family had replenished the earth. God had caused different people to speak different languages because they were trying to reach heaven by their own works to honor themselves. God proceeds to reveal *His* way to heaven.

Read Scripture

Genesis 12:1–8

Questions

Genesis 12:1

AGES 3–8 A Who told Abram to leave his country and family?

AGES 9–14 B Does God tell Abram the place he is to go?

ADULT C Are all the details told Abram before the Lord sees he is going to obey?

Genesis 12:2, 3

A Do you think Abram would like to be blessed by God and be a helper or blessing to other people? Would you?

B Who says He will make Abram famous and blessed? Does Abram have to work hard to do it?

C Is there room for fear for Abram? Who takes full responsibility for the results of obedience.

Genesis 12:4, 5

A Did Abram go alone to the land of Canaan?

B Did Abram take relatives with him? Who else went?

C Did Abram do everything God told him to do? What did he do that is questionable? Was he openly disobedient?

Genesis 12:6, 7

A When Abram came to the land of Canaan, were there other people living there?

B Does God tell Abram what place He will give him for his future family? What difficulty seems to be in the way?

C In what way can you see Abram trusting God for the outcome of this problem of an already inhabited land being promised to him? What act indicates this?

Genesis 12:8

A What kind of a house does Abram live in? Can it be moved easily? Does Abram know the Lord sees him wherever he moves?

B Tell how you picture Abram moving from the flat land to the mountains.

C What seems to be very important each time Abram moves? Do you see an example for us in Abram's actions?

Conclusion

Abram is a man showing faith in God by obeying. To obey fully, he realizes he must keep in constant communication with the Lord. He was not perfect, but God saw his desire to obey and his love shown by the worship at the altars.

Prayer

Suggestion

Find a map (perhaps in your Bible) with the mentioned areas and towns.

GOD MAKES A COVENANT WITH BELIEVING ABRAHAM—GENESIS 15:1–5; 17:1–19

13

Prayer

The leader is encouraged to pray that each member of the family will have a deep and lasting desire to obey God.

Let's Read God's Word

Genesis 15:1–5; 17:1–19

Let's Talk About What We Have Read

What is the beautiful way that God told Abraham about His plans?

Did Abraham's faith please God?

What is the covenant promise that God made with Abraham?

What was Abraham's part of the contract?

How did God plan to give Abraham a son?

Let's Remember What We Have Read

1 God chose Abraham to be His special servant.

2 Abraham responded in obedience and faith.

3 God rewarded his faith by establishing a covenant that would last through the centuries.

Prayer

Dear Lord, we thank You for the way in which You still seek people today to be Your own through the new covenant of the blood of Jesus Christ. Give us hearts like Abraham's, willing to respond in obedience to You. *Amen.*

ABRAHAM—GENESIS 18:1–16

(The Revised Standard Version is used in this lesson.)

14

Prayer

Open with a prayer of thanks for this portion of Scripture. Pray that we may have the faith of Abraham and his great desire to follow and please God.

Introduction

Let us recall that Abraham was called by God to leave his home in Ur of the Chaldees to go to a land that God would show him. God promised to make him a great nation (Genesis 12:1–3). The sign of the covenant between God and Abraham was circumcision of all males in Abraham's household (Genesis 17:10–14). In Genesis 16, his son Ishmael is born. However, God reveals to Abraham that a son will be born to him through Sarah (Genesis 17:16, 19).

Read Scripture

Genesis 18:1–16

Questions

1 Who appeared to Abraham? (Note how royally the guests were treated.)

2 What was the message given to Abraham concerning Sarah?

3 Where was Sarah, and what was she doing?

4 What was Sarah's reaction to the message?

5 What does verse 18:14 reveal to us?

6 Was it a sin for Sarah to laugh? Or, was it her denial of the laughter that was sinful? (Read Proverbs 6:16, 17.)

7 Where did the men go?

Food for Thought

1 Do you think that Abraham realized who his guests were? Consider Matthew 25:35 and Hebrews 13:2. Can you re-

call showing hospitality to strangers? What are your thoughts and feelings about these verses and the subject as a whole?

2 We can wonder if Sarah already knew of God's revelation to Abraham, that she would bear a son and call him Isaac (Genesis 17:16, 19). Why do you think she laughed? Until now, all of God's dealings had been primarily with Abraham. Could it be that Sarah may have been sitting on the sidelines just observing, not truly giving in to belief in this God of Abraham? Remember that they had come from Ur which was known to be a center of idol worship. Each of us must have faith of our own in the God of Abraham. We, too, may have laughed to think that a woman ninety years old was going to have a child. In Hebrews 11:16, we learn specifically that Sarah by faith received power to conceive, even when she was past the normal childbearing age, since she considered God faithful to do what He had promised. When it is God's will, ". . . with God all things are possible." Mark 10:27 and Genesis 18:14 give us this basic truth.

Prayer

ABRAHAM—GENESIS 18:16–33 (Continued)

(The Revised Standard Version is used in this study.)

15

Prayer

Open the study with thankfulness for this portion of Scripture and ask for guidance in understanding.

Read Scripture

Questions

1 Who were these men? According to our previous lesson and Genesis 19:1, we gain insight into their identity.
2 Why did the Lord want to reveal His plan to Abraham?
3 What were the conditions Abraham had to follow in order "that the Lord may bring to Abraham what he has promised him"?
4 What do we learn about the cities of Sodom and Gomorrah here?
5 For how many righteous people is the Lord willing to spare Sodom from destruction?
6 When did the Lord leave Abraham?

Food for Thought

1 How available do you feel the Lord is to you? Is He as accessible to us today as in the days of Abraham? How do you know this?
2 In other parts of the Bible, Abraham is mentioned as God's friend (2 Chronicles 20:7 and Isaiah 41:8). Do the verses we are studying today (Genesis 18:16–33) reveal the very close relationship and understanding between Abraham and God?
3 Do you feel that it is our responsibility to intercede in prayer for the world around us, as Abraham did for Sodom? Specifically, what are you concerned about to bring before the Lord in prayer?

Prayer

GOD TESTS ABRAHAM'S FAITH—GENESIS 22:1–18

16

Prayer

Dear Father, teach us to have faith enough to trust You when the situation seems impossible. *Amen.*

Let's Read God's Word

Let's Talk About What We Have Read

Why did God test Abraham by asking him to sacrifice Isaac?

Can someone tell the rest of the story in his own words?

What was the question Isaac asked Abraham as they walked together to the place of sacrifice?

How did Abraham answer him?

What makes you believe Abraham really meant this?

How was Abraham stopped from killing Isaac?

How did God provide another sacrifice?

What was God's overwhelming response to Abraham's obedience?

What can we learn from this about God's response to a believing heart?

Let's Remember What We Have Read

1 God tested Abraham to see if he really put the Lord first.
2 When God saw how Abraham trusted and obeyed Him, even to sacrificing his own son, He blessed him beyond measure.

Prayer

Let each one pray silently that God would teach him to have more trust in some specific area of life.

GENESIS 24:1–4, 10–27, 50, 51

17

Prayer

Read Scripture

Questions

1 What is Abraham's concern? Why?
2 Why does he not go and look for a wife for his son, Isaac? Whom does he send?
3 What kind of a man is the servant?
4 How does he expect to be able to find a good wife for Isaac?
5 What do these verses tell you about Rebekah?
6 What do these verses tell you about God?
7 Do you think God guides people in specific ways these days? Do you know of someone who has been guided? Have you?

FOR TEEN-AGERS Read Genesis 26:34, 35

If Abraham went to lots of trouble seeking a particular wife for Isaac to protect him from the Canaanite religion and customs, what do you think *your parents'* responsibility is in this area? Why? What importance in your life does picking a girl/boy-friend have? Should you date a non-Christian if you are a Christian? Why? Should you marry a non-Christian if you are a believer? Why?

Prayer

Dear Lord, we thank You for the special interest You take in all our affairs. We are grateful that whoever we are, *You* consider us special just as Abraham and Sarah considered Isaac special. Please help us to remember that fact all the time. And thanks for this example of Isaac's faith, a son who did not just depend on his father's faith but had his own living faith in God! *Amen.*

GENESIS 25:19–34

(Use the Living Bible for this study.)

18

Prayer

Read Scripture

Now Take Turns Filling in the Blanks

Just as Abraham and Sarah had to wait and trust God for Isaac, Isaac and Rebekah were married for twenty years before God answered *his* prayer. Isaac was _____ years old when he became the father of t_______. Isaac had p_______ for God to give Rebekah a child. She became pregnant. Then she asked God what was happening because it seemed as if the children were f_______ in her womb!

God told Rebekah: One will be _________.

The older will serve the _________.

They will be r_________.

Jacob, who was the younger twin, came out, "grabbing" his brother's heel. A baby's natural instinct to grasp whatever touches its palm had much significance in this birth incident.

Questions

Where did Rebekah come from?

How did the parents feel about their sons? Why?

Did Esau value being the oldest?

What is the birthright? (Have someone look it up in the dictionary.)

Challenge Question (Older children, adults)

In this passage, we read that the twins *seemed to fight in the womb.* The Lord told Rebekah their personalities were present already; they would be rivals. We cannot build too heavily on this but should consider what it means in terms of taking fetal life at random. Discuss abortion.

Prayer

Father in Heaven, take some of the thoughts we have found in Your Word and use them to teach us today. We know Your Word is able to reach us where we are. Teach us about prayer, too. In Jesus' Name. *Amen.*

GENESIS 25

19

Prayer

Introduction

Even though Abraham had many other children, Isaac was given all that his father had because he was special. It would be through Isaac that God's special things would continue.

Read Scripture

Genesis 25:12–18

Questions

Did God bless Ishmael? (*See* 17:20 and 21:13.)

Who are Ishmael's children today? How important are the Arabs today in God's eyes?

What should be our attitude toward them after reading these Scriptures?

Drama for Genesis 25:29–34 Living Bible (optional)

Let one child be Jacob, and one be Esau, and read the story out loud, with verses 29, 33b and 34 read by the father. Talk about what actually occurred, that after the trade Jacob became number one in the family. Also, Esau was indifferent to his loss as God had known he would be even before he was born (verse 23). Talk about how God knows *everything* about us and cares for us. (*See* Psalms 139:1–5.)

Discussion Questions

With your children, discuss how special each child in your family is. Compare this to Isaac's arrival—how each was anticipated, enjoyed, loved—express verbally each child's strengths and what he adds to the family. (NOTE: Parents should be honest here—examining their attitudes to their children first; if some of your attitudes are negative about your child, then face them and decide how it can be discussed truthfully.)

Prayer

Dear Father, we thank You that we have the relationship of sons and daughters to You. Speak to us today through these Words as a Father, kind and firm. *Amen.*

GENESIS 26:1–17
(Living Bible)

20

Prayer

Introduction

God continues to deal with and bless men through His promise to Abraham and now *Isaac*, the promised heir.

Read the Scripture

Questions

Why did Isaac move to Gerar? (This city is about forty miles west of Hebron; it has been located by archaeologists.)

Give the parts of God's promise to Isaac.

Why would King Abimelech be afraid to hurt Isaac or Rebekah?

Now read verses 28, 29.

What do these say about the king's knowledge of Isaac's God?

Where do you think he learned about Isaac's God?

Let's read about wells: Verses 18–32. (Wells mean water and water means life. No one can live without water, whether it pours out of faucets or collects in precious wells in the desert.)

Now read the Scripture passage.

What did Isaac do?

Find the four wells by name, and see if you can tell the story of their names.

In Genesis 26, God appears two times. Can you find these appearances?

Food for Thought

It is amazing to see the similarities between Jesus and Isaac.

	ISAAC	*JESUS*
1	Promised Seed of Abraham (Genesis 7:19)	Promised Seed of Abraham (Matthew 1:1)
2	Trusted his father (Genesis 22:9)	Trusted His Father (John 8: 28, 29)
3	Protected by his father from bad influences (Genesis 24:4; 21:10–12)	Protected by His Father from death (Matthew 2:13–15)
4	Only beloved son given for sacrifice (Genesis 22:12, 16; Hebrews 11:17, 18)	Only Beloved Son given for sacrifice (John 3:16; Romans 8:32)

5	Silent sacrifice (Genesis 22:9)	Silent sacrifice (Isaiah 53:7)
6	Raised in Abraham's mind (Hebrews 11:19)	Raised from the dead! (Matthew 28:5, 6)

Prayer

Dear Lord, it is fantastic to think that a promise You made to Abraham and Isaac hundreds—oh, thousands of years ago—is for us because we are the people that are now blessed through them . . . we know about Jesus. Thank You, Lord! *Amen.*

THE CASE OF THE CAVE CALLED MACH-PELAH—GENESIS 25

(Use Living Bible in this study.)

21

Prayer

Read Scripture

Genesis 25:9, 10

Questions

After reading this little paragraph, you might think that the Cave of Mach-pelah was just a scary grave. It was the place where Isaac buried his father, Abraham. The Bible says that Abraham bought a piece of land and this cave for 400 pieces of silver to bury Sarah, his wife. But the Bible keeps talking about this cave! Wonder why?

CLUE 1 Check out Genesis 23:16–20 (permanent possession).
CLUE 2 Proceed to Genesis 35:29 Where was Isaac buried?
CLUE 3 Genesis 49:29–31 Where was Jacob when he said this?
CLUE 4 Genesis 50:5 Where was the Cave?

Again, and again God wrote about the Cave; even Stephen talks about it in the New Testament (Acts 7:15, 16). And Joseph made them promise to take his bones there from Egypt (Hebrews 11:22).

So we see that from Abraham, the Father of the Jews, right on down the line to Isaac, Jacob, and Joseph, everyone was insistent upon being buried in the Cave of Mach-pelah in Canaan. Even when it meant all the family making the trip from Egypt up to Canaan when Jacob died.

Here's the Answer to the Riddle of the Cave

For a smart guy like Abraham to buy a cave way down in Canaan made no sense at all; he never owned or belonged to that land. Except for one thing—*God* had told him someday the whole land of Canaan would be his and his sons'! Abraham, Isaac, and Jacob believed He would do what He said. He would bring the Jews to the Promised Land, Canaan. So-o-o-o they buried all their family in the cave there in Canaan waiting until all the land was theirs! They did not know when, but they knew they would one day return. They believed God's promise. What faith!

Sing or read

Charles Wesley's old hymn, "Father of Jesus Christ, my Lord."

Faith, Mighty Faith, the promise sees, and looks to that alone;
Laughs at impossibilities, and cries it shall be done!
And cries it shall, it shall be done,
Laughs at impossibilities, and cries it shall be done!

Prayer

Pray that we have Abraham's faith.

GENESIS 27

(Use Living Bible in this study.)

22

Prayer

Scripture Reading

Genesis 27 (Assign different family members a "role" and let each one read his part.)

Discussion

Rebekah's and Jacob's deception in light of the fact that God had intended Jacob to have the blessing all along.

The blessing conferred on Jacob. (*See* Genesis 12:1–3; 26:3, 4, 24 and 25:23 for the promise originally given to Abraham and then passed on to his descendents.)

Esau's reaction, remembering that he had willingly sold his birthright to Jacob (Genesis 25:33).

CROSS-REFERENCES Hebrews 11:20; 12:15–17.

Drama (optional)

In your own words, act out this Scripture chapter. Characters —Isaac and Rebekah, Jacob and Esau.

Prayer

Ask God to help us trust Him to work out His plan for our lives rather than scheme or connive to get what we want.

THE BEGINNING OF JACOB'S WALK WITH GOD—GENESIS 28:10–22

23

Prayer

Introduction

Jacob has deceived his father Isaac into giving him the blessing that was by birth the blessing of Esau, Jacob's older twin. To get away from Esau's anger, Jacob is sent to his uncle Laban's house to pick a wife.

Read Scripture

Questions

Genesis 28:10, 11

AGES 3–8 A When the sun is set what time of day is it? Does darkness scare you?

AGES 9–13 B What type of country do you picture from these verses?

ADULT C What do you imagine were the thoughts of Jacob?

Genesis 28:12–15

A Who *talked* to Jacob in his dream?

B Describe the setting of this scene. What does the Lord say about the land where Jacob is sleeping?

C Restate this promise from God to Jacob (list at least five different parts). What previously studied men heard a similar promise?

Genesis 28:16, 17

A Why did Jacob say he was afraid of this place?

B Why would Jacob be afraid to be in God's house?

C What seems to be a discrepancy from what Jacob feels and what God said just before he awoke?

Genesis 28:18, 19 (NOTE: *Bethel* means house of God.)

A Have you ever put a stick or stone in the ground to mark a certain place that you want to go back to later?

B From his actions, do you think Jacob believed his dream was a real truth?

C From his actions, reiterate what promise from God Jacob is showing he believes.

Genesis 28:20–22

A Who made the promise or vow in these verses? Did God make the same promise back a few verses?

B What is Jacob's answer to God's promises? Does he seem to be willing to do what God wants?

C Very briefly trace Jacob's reactions or actions through this entire passage (28:10–22). What action is the last mentioned? Can we show belief by our actions?

Conclusion

Jacob, as a sinful man, realizes the Presence of God and is afraid, but, when he believes God, his fear is changed to obedience and worship. God offers the same opportunity to all people.

Prayer

GENESIS 28

24

Prayer

Scripture Reading

Questions

CHILDREN Where did Isaac send Jacob? To do what?
Tell about Jacob's dream.

TEEN-AGERS What was the real reason for Jacob's leaving home?
Why did Esau marry a daughter of Ishmael? Who was Ishmael?

ADULTS What was the significance of Jacob's dream?
Explain how God's blessing on Jacob was both national and personal in scope.

Discussion

Contrast Jacob's self-seeking actions as recorded in chapter 27 with his reaction to God's appearance to him in his dream.

Prayer

Singing (optional)

Choose a song about God's promise to guide and direct the lives of those who put their trust in Him.

GENESIS 29:1–31

(Use The Revised Standard Version.)

25

Prayer

Scripture Reading

True or False

1 Jacob traveled until he came to the home of his mother's relatives.

2 Jacob helped Rachel water her father's sheep.
3 Laban wanted Jacob to return home as soon as possible.
4 Jacob fell in love with Leah.
5 Rachel was the oldest daughter and therefore married Jacob first.
6 Jacob married his second wife one week after the first.
7 It was the custom of Paddan-aram, where Hara was situated, to marry off the oldest daughter first.

Discussion

Jacob deceived Isaac, his father, to obtain the blessing. Now Laban, his father-in-law, has deceived him. What might Jacob now think about his actions?

Genesis 29:31 How did the Lord look upon this polygamous marriage? It must be noted here that later it was forbidden to marry two sisters in each other's lifetime, according to Leviticus 18:18 RSV. (Leah's situation was pathetic to say the least. However, Leah was honored by the Lord by being allowed to become the mother of Levi and Judah. From them arose the priestly and royal Messianic tribes of Israel, respectively.)

Drama (optional)

Let two members of the family secretly select one incident from this Scripture portion and portray it in charade. How long does it take the other members of the family to guess it correctly?

Prayer

Close with a prayer of thanksgiving for this portion of Scripture. Pray to be led and guided in our daily tasks.

(Suggested Reading: *The Old Testament Speaks* by Samuel J. Schultz.)

GENESIS 31:1–29

(The Revised Standard Version is used in this study.)

26

Prayer

Read Scripture

Questions

1 What were the sons of Laban saying about Jacob (Genesis 31:1)?
2 How had Laban's affections for Jacob changed (Genesis 31:2)?

3 In addition to Laban's disfavor, how was Jacob encouraged to return home to his father (Genesis 31:3, 16)?
4 What were Rachel's and Leah's reaction to Jacob's decision to return to his homeland?
5 Did God note how Laban treated Jacob?
6 How did God seem to rectify the situation?
7 What did Jacob take with him when he left Paddan-aram (Genesis 31:17)?
8 Had Jacob revealed his plans to Laban?
9 What was Laban's reaction to the news that Jacob had fled?
10 Laban must have been very angry with Jacob, to say the least. How did God protect Jacob from Laban (Genesis 31:24, 29)?

Food for Thought

1 In Genesis 31:36, does Laban have reason to be angry with Jacob? How could their relationship have been different? Compare their relationship to that of Abraham and Lot when they divided land in Genesis 13:8–12. How did selfishness and greed affect both men's lives? Think of Jacob's earlier life. Does Proverbs 15:27 speak to us today? Do you know of anyone with whom this Proverb has proved to be true? Was it true in Laban's and Jacob's lives? How?
2 Jacob certainly made errors of judgment in his life; we can look at them and try to avoid the same mistakes. God looked upon Jacob as faithful and promised him that He would be with him (Genesis 28:15 and 31:3). Can we expect the same kind of protection and guidance that Jacob experienced? Can you give an example?

Prayer

GENESIS 32:1–30

(The Revised Standard Version is used in this study.)

27

Prayer

Read Scripture

Questions

1 To what place was Jacob traveling?
2 Who met him while he was on his way? Note that God

had directed him to return to his homeland (Genesis 31:3). When Jacob obeyed God's command, he was met and, more than likely, encouraged by the angels of the Lord.

3 How did Jacob inform his brother Esau of his arrival?
4 What did the messengers have to tell Jacob when they returned from Esau?
5 How did Jacob react, and what did he imagine Esau's plans to be?
6 What was Jacob's only hope?
7 In desperation, to what did Jacob resort (Genesis 32:9–12)?
8 What part of Jacob's character is revealed here (Genesis 32:10)? Have we seen this facet of his personality before?
9 In Jacob's prayer, what promises of God did he recall? Up to this point in Jacob's life, he had always come out on top of every crisis.
10 What was Jacob's deep fear? Recall that Esau had threatened to kill him (Genesis 27:41).
11 How did Jacob hope to appease his brother?
12 After arranging to be left alone, what happened to Jacob?
13 When did Jacob know for sure who the Man was?
14 What was Jacob's request of the Man?
15 In addition to the request, to what was Jacob's name changed?
16 In Genesis 32:26, why was the Man so anxious to leave before daybreak? This is another clue as to His identity. In Exodus 33:20, Moses was told that he could not see God's face: ". . . for man shall not see me and live." The Bible is its own interpreter. When we find a difficult text, we can usually find one to explain it.

Discussion

Contrast Jacob's present attitude toward his brother with his former attitude toward him. How do we in our family feel and act toward one another? On an international scale, what is the root cause of wars?

CROSS-REFERENCE Read 1 John 2:4–11 about loving one another.

Prayer

Prayer is one expression of love for one another. Pray for each other. Ask God to put His love in our hearts.

GOD RENEWS HIS COVENANT WITH JACOB—GENESIS 35:9–19

28

Prayer

Let's Read God's Word

Genesis 35:9–19

Let's Talk About What We Have Read

Who were Jacob's father and grandfather?
What new name did God give Jacob?
What did that new name mean?
Why do you think God gave Jacob a new name?
In verse 11, how did God describe Himself to Jacob?
What did God then say He would do for Jacob?
What promise did God make to Jacob's grandfather?
What name do we give these promises of God?
What did Jacob do after God told him His great plan?

Discussion

Remembering that the name Jacob means "supplanter" and Israel means "one who has persevered with the Lord," what does the renaming and blessing of Jacob indicate?

Let's Remember What We Have Read

1 This lesson reminds us how faithful God is to His covenant promise.
2 We can see through this lesson that God uses the family as one means of preserving His truth for coming generations.

Prayer

Sing or say the words to "Faith of Our Fathers."

(Reference Material: *Notes on the Pentateuch: Genesis to Deuteronomy* by C. H. Mackintosh.)

GENESIS 37:1–4, 12–28

29

Prayer

Read Scripture

Jacob was Abraham's grandson and Isaac's son. Now he is a father himself, with twelve strong sons.

Questions

1 Of all his sons, who was Jacob's favorite?
2 How did the brothers feel about Joseph? For any reasons?
3 When Joseph went to find his shepherd brothers, what did they think of at once?
4 What was their plan?
5 Who had a better idea? What was it?
6 Who had still another idea? What was it?
7 How do you think the brothers felt as they saw the camels and men disappear in the distance? How do you think Joseph felt?
8 Do you think that unpleasant things may sometimes be a part of God's good plan? Can you think of any examples?

Prayer

(Suggested Reading for Children: *My Brother's Keeper,* Spire Christian Comics.)

FACING TEMPTATION—GENESIS 39:1–23

30

Prayer

Please give us understanding today, Father, in Your Word.

Read Scripture

Young (seventeen-year-old) Joseph is now about 500 miles from his home and family, in a strange land with strange ways and a strange language. The Ishmaelites had bought him; now they sell him.

Questions

1 Who bought the young man?
2 What was the only comfort Joseph had in this dismal situation? Who else recognized this fact? Do you think anyone notices by your life that God is with you?
3 Verse 5: Do you think any of the blessings your family enjoys are because of someone else—a godly grandparent or great-grandparent? Read also Genesis 26:17, 24, and 30:27.
4 A great temptation came to this handsome young man: his master's wife begged him to act very wrongly. What was his response to her urgings? What was the main reason he would not do as she asked?
5 Why did the master's wife make up this lie about Joseph?

Did his master believe her? What might he have done with his young Hebrew slave? What did he do? (Joseph was placed in the one prison in Egypt that gave access to King Pharaoh.) (*See* verse 20.)

6 How would you feel if you ended up in prison for doing the right thing? Would you feel God was with you?

Prayer

The family may wish to sing the hymn "Yield Not to Temptation" by H. R. Palmer.

DEPENDENCE ON GOD—GENESIS 41:1–16

31

Prayer

Father, we read that spiritual things can only be understood by the help of the Holy Spirit. Please let Him be our Teacher today.

Introduction

Joseph, a slave of an Egyptian captain, was put in prison because of a lie of an evil woman. Read Psalms 105:17–19 and Genesis 39:20–23 and describe Joseph's life in prison. Does Psalms 105:19 give you any clue why God may have permitted this to happen to Joseph even after he had done the right thing?

Read Scripture

Genesis 41:1–16

Questions

1 This passage begins by telling us that the powerful king of Egypt had two dreams. How did they affect him? What were the dreams? What did he want to know?

2 Who couldn't solve the king's problem? Who had a helpful idea? What was it?

3 How long was Joseph in prison? Do you think he was tempted to feel God had forgotten him? How do you think he felt when he was told the king wanted him?

4 What does Joseph's response to the king tell you about Joseph?

5 What can you do that God has enabled you to do?

Prayer

Dear Lord, please help us not to take the credit for what You have given to us. *Amen.*

GENESIS 41:17–40

32

Prayer

So many distractions draw our minds and hearts away from You and Your Word, Father. Please help us to give attention to this lesson today.

Read Scripture

Can you picture this scene: the great king of Egypt, probably on a magnificent throne, desperately hoping a young Hebrew slave (just out of prison) can help him? Does Joseph seem overcome by the grandeur of the situation—or the danger? What if he fails?

Questions

1 After Pharaoh related his dreams, what did God do? What did Joseph do?
2 Since Pharaoh didn't believe in the true God, it may have surprised him to hear that his dreams were a message from God. What was the message?
3 What did Joseph suggest the king do about this disaster which was coming on the country?
4 What was the king's response to all this?
5 Did Joseph ask for any favor from the king for interpreting the dream? What might he have asked for? How was he favored? Why?
6 If God does not speak to people through dreams now, how does He speak to us?

Prayer

Dear Lord, please help us to take Your message to us seriously. *Amen.*

FORGIVENESS—GENESIS 45:1–28

33

Prayer

Father, the psalmist said Your Word is more precious than gold. Help us so to value it in our family.

Introduction

Joseph's brothers came to Egypt the second time for food for their starving families. Though they had seen and talked to

Joseph, they did not recognize him. But the time came when Joseph could no longer keep his secret.

Read Scripture

Questions

1 How did Joseph feel when he revealed who he was? How did his brothers feel? Why?
2 Who did Joseph say was responsible for his being in Egypt? For what purpose?
3 Pick out all the references Joseph made to God's control of his life.
4 Besides forgiveness, what else did Joseph offer his brothers? Did the king approve of this plan? To what extent?
5 How do you think old father Jacob felt when the brothers returned with donkeys loaded with grain and extra "good things of Egypt" and told him, "Joseph is still alive, and he is ruler over all the land of Egypt" (RSV)?
6 What about Joseph's life helps you as you think about the future?

Prayer

Dear Lord, we thank You that You are always in control of even difficult situations in our lives. *Amen.*

JACOB FORETELLS THE FUTURE OF HIS CHILDREN—GENESIS 49:1–33

34

Prayer

Pray that the Holy Spirit will instruct the hearts of your family through this lesson.

Let's Read God's Word

Genesis 49:1–33

Let's Talk About What We Have Read

Why did Jacob call his sons together?

Did Jacob say that all of his sons would be blessed and live fruitful lives?

Name two whose lives would not be full of blessing.

Why were they not blessed?

We know that Jacob was a man who was greatly blessed by God and yet some of his sons were not living to please God. What can we learn from this?

What did Jacob say about Joseph?

Did Joseph's faith in God have anything to do with the blessings he was to receive?

What was Jacob's prophecy concerning Judah?

What could the word *Shiloh* in verse 10 refer to?

Let's Remember What We Have Read

1 The prophecies of Jacob concerning his twelve sons (the tribes of Israel) were directly linked to the kinds of lives the sons were living.

2 Even in Jacob's house, each son had to determine for himself whether or not he wished to live for God.

3 From Jacob's blessing on Judah, we see that God intended to continue His covenant line through Jacob's family as He had promised.

Prayer

Our loving Heavenly Father, keep each of us in this family close to You. We pray that You will see fit through Your Holy Spirit to open each of our hearts to the reality of Jesus Christ as Saviour and Lord of our lives. *Amen.*

GENESIS 50:1–6, 14–26

35

Prayer

Father, we offer the prayer of young Samuel, "Speak, Lord, for thy servant hears" (1 Samuel 3:9 RSV).

Introduction

This is the closing chapter of the Book of Genesis, and the closing chapter of Joseph's life. He was a great man, because God was with him.

Read Scripture

Questions

1 Joseph's elderly father died in the foreign land, Egypt. What promise did Joseph make to him before he died? Why was this so important to him? (Read Genesis 49:29–31.)

2 Do you have any ideas why Joseph did not arrange for all of his family to return at this time and stay in Canaan? (*See* Genesis 48:21.)

3 After the burial, and the family is again in Egypt, what do the brothers fear? Why?

4 How did Joseph react to their request? What did he say to them? Why is it usually hard to forgive people?

5 As Joseph grew older, what did he request of his brothers? Did they carry out his wishes? (*See also* Joshua 24:32.)

6 What do the events in Joseph's life tell you about God? (Let each member of the family give one idea.)

Prayer

Dear Lord, please help us to have a spirit of forgiveness like Joseph toward people who wrong us. *Amen.*

CREATION—OPEN-BOOK QUIZ—GENESIS 1:1–25

(Find the answers in the Living Bible.)

1

"In the beginning God created the heaven and the earth" (Genesis 1:1–25 KJV).

This must be the most simple and yet complex statement ever written! In what order do we read about God's Creation? Let's look at the steps and fill in the missing words.

First, with the Spirit of God brooding over the dark ______, there was l______ which God divided from d______.

Second, He divided the sky and ______ below.

Third, then God created p______ and t______ which bore s______.

Fourth, when we sunbathe, sleep out under the stars, or share a full moon, we can understand why God was ______ with this part of Creation! Then ______ and ______ were ordered to replenish the earth. Did they? Now put on your thinking cap: See how many reptiles and wild animals you can name.

True or False

In God's Creation, each new day depended on the one before it.

The order of Creation wasn't important.

Discuss

What if man had been created first?

CREATION—OPEN-BOOK QUIZ—GENESIS 1:14–25

2

True or False

1 The sun and moon were not created to give light on the earth.
2 The sun, moon, and stars mark off the days, seasons, and years.
3 Fish were the first kind of animal to be made.

4 God commanded the fish and birds to stay few in number.
5 Animals were made out of the ground.
6 Animals were created originally according to species.

Discussion for Teen-agers

According to the Theory of Evolution, in ancient times some very simple one-celled creatures began to change—some into plants and some into animals. This change continues producing descendants with new characteristics from generation to generation, going from lower to higher forms. The biblical fact of Creation is that God made the world by separate acts, creating man, animals, and plants out of nothing. Each could only reproduce within its own species. "Let the earth bring forth the living creature after his kind . . ." (Genesis 1:24). To believe that man is in the process of evolving from a lower state is to deny (1) Bible as historical fact (2) God as the Creator (3) The reality of sin and the need for personal redemption from sin. (In other words, if man is still evolving, sin, as we know it, is "mere imperfection" which will disappear at a later time.)

Discuss the fact of biblical Creation versus the Theory of Evolution.

What should we do or say when confronted at school with Darwinism?

(For further study: *Journey Away From God* by Robert Benedict.)

CREATION—OPEN-BOOK QUIZ— GENESIS 1:26–31; 2:7–25

3

Creation of Man

After God had made a certain environment on earth (light, air, water, creatures, and plant life), He placed man there. Fill in the blanks describing man and the Garden.

Man and woman were made in the image of ________.

God said man was to be the master of all life in the ________, ________, and ________.

Man's body was formed from ________ of the ________.

The breath of life comes from ________.

The four rivers of the Garden were ________

____

____

________.

At the center of the Garden there were two special trees: ————, ————.

True or False

1 Even though Adam had the fellowship of God, the company of all the animals, and plenty to eat, God still thought Adam needed a helper.
2 God made Eve the same way He made Adam.
3 Eve named all the animals.

Discuss

How are men and women different from the other things God made?

CREATION WORSHIP SERVICE FOR THE FAMILY

(Living Bible, King James Version; Genesis 2:1–3; Psalm 8)

As Genesis 2:1–3 and Psalm 8 are read, the family can be inspired to worship through praise, prayer, sharing, and song.

Praise

FATHER	In response to what the Bible says, our family should *praise* God for His Works. He gives each of us life-power through Creation. Each one of us is created different. He has never made another person just like you. Each new baby is completely different, even in the same family.
MOTHER	Our Creator, the Bible says in the Psalm that the children will praise You.
FIRST CHILD	Your name is excellent in all the earth.
SECOND CHILD	You made the heavens, the sun and moon, Venus, Mars, the Milky Way, and millions of stars.
MOTHER	When the heavens and earth were finished, You rested on the seventh day.
FATHER	Best of all, You made us to take care of all the other creatures and all of Creation—the plants and trees, the animals, birds, and fish—like the zebra, the bear, dogs and cats, turtles, cows, the camel, ostrich, shark, whale, lobster, crabs, and salmon.
MOTHER	God gave us an example by resting on the seventh day. Don't we, too, need to set aside one day a week for different activity and rest?

Song of Praise

"All Things Bright and Beautiful" by Cecil Frances Alexander, or "How Great Thou Art" by Stuart K. Hine.

Sharing

Share together some thoughts on God's Creation. For example, father, mother, and the older children can share scientific knowledge about man's makeup, or about the wonders of the earth and sea and space. The little ones can be encouraged to discuss pretty things they see outside. Or they can discuss how important their eyes, ears, feet, and hands are; or how wonderful it is to be able to smell, taste, feel, talk, and walk! Have them even *do* some of these to experience it.

Prayer and Praise

Father should close with praise and thanksgiving for what has been shared.

Studies in Proverbs

Solomon, the son of David, was not only a great king but an esteemed scientist, philosopher, poet, architect, and businessman as well. The reason: he had been given the gift of wisdom by God. We read in 1 Kings 4:29–32 that God gave him "wisdom and understanding . . . largeness of heart . . . he was wiser than all men . . . he spake three thousand proverbs."

Although Solomon is usually said to be the author of this book, very probably he collected the proverbs. Some were copied by men of Hezekiah's time; some were written by Agur and some by King Lemuel. It is believed that they were written between 1000 and 700 B.C. to the Jewish nation.

The Book of Proverbs has been described as "a guide to right living"; it shows us how to put God into everyday life and gives instructions on dealing with the practical affairs of this world. In modern parlance, it's a how-to book.

Webster describes a proverb as "a short, pithy sentence expressing a truth ascertained by experience or observation." Teaching by proverbs is one of the oldest forms of instruction because this method was appealing to the oriental mind. (Example: Confucius's saying, "To go beyond is as wrong as to fall short.")

Proverbs is different from the other Books of the Bible that your family is studying in this edition of *The Family Bible Study Book*. Therefore, it is being approached not on a chapter by chapter basis but on subject matter or theme. Basic truths and teachings run throughout Proverbs, and our various authors have taken different approaches to the universal truths this book of wisdom contains. You may want to start with the first lesson and continue consecutively; or you may want to skip around, finding topics your family is particularly interested in. This section contains a number of lessons especially for teen-agers because it is thought that originally the Book of Proverbs was designed as a school book for the instruction of young men.

In his Pocket Bible Handbook, Henry H. Halley lists twenty-nine subjects that are covered in Proverbs. Other commentaries provide still different categories. For the purposes of this study, we have twelve topics or themes. In alphabetical order they are: Chastity and Adultery, Control of the Tongue, Diligence and Laziness, Drunkenness and Temperance, Friends and Enemies, Good and Evil, Guidelines for Family Life, Honesty and Lying, Riches and Poverty, Self-Control, Wisdom and Common Sense, and finally Quizzes. Where the lesson is based on selections from Proverbs, it is listed under the first selection. A complete list of themes or topics appears in the general index in the back of the book. This index includes not only the themes from Proverbs but from the other books being studied as well.

As you read Proverbs with your family, consider how little the nature of man has changed in 3,000 years! Consider how the wisdom of Solomon—which came directly from God—has as much meaning in this century as it did in 1000 B.C.

CHASTITY AND ADULTERY
(This section for teens and adults.)

PROVERBS 5:1–14

1

Prayer

Father, we ask You to please instruct us in Your Word just now.

From the time a child is small, parents try to warn him about danger: "Don't touch the stove or you'll get burned." "Don't cross the streets without looking or you'll get hit." Small children usually accept such warnings. After adolescence there are special dangers for our children, and parents would be remiss not to give warnings then.

Read Scripture

Questions

1 Solomon is dealing with a timeless youthful temptation: sexual immorality. How does he express his plea for his son to follow his advice?

2 Though this passage speaks of a young man being lured into sin by a girl, the teaching is equally applicable to a girl who is being tempted by a young man. What characterizes the invitation to sin (7:5; 5:3, *also* 7:21)?
3 How does the offer of the temptress appear (7:16–18)?
4 How does she assure the young man that "no one will ever know" (7:19, 20)? Is this not usually a factor in a moment of temptation?
5 What factors contributed to the young man's participation in this sin (7:7, 8, 22)?
6 The thing that had looked so attractive turned out in what way (7:22, 23, 26 and 5:4–15)? (Very likely 5:11 refers to venereal disease, as the Living Bible suggests.)
7 What would have saved this young man (will save you) from yielding to strong temptation (5:8; 7:25; 7:15)?

Prayer

Thank You, dear Father, for the beautiful gift of sexual love which You designed for the relationship of marriage. Please help us to resist any temptation to use this gift out of Your will. *Amen.*

CHASTITY AND ADULTERY

THE PROSTITUTE—PROVERBS 5:1–23

2

Opening Prayer

Scripture Reading

Questions

1 Why must one listen to good counsel in verse 2?
2 Where does a prostitute lead a man? Why (verse 6)?
3 How does a prostitute draw a man to her? What happens afterward?
4 In verses 7–14, for what reasons are young men admonished to stay away from prostitutes?
5 How important is your reputation to you? Why should we care as Christians how we appear to others?
6 Why should a man be faithful to his wife?
7 In verse 21, who watches every move you make?
8 What will happen to those that commit adultery? Why?

Closing Prayer

CHASTITY AND ADULTERY

ADULTERY—PROVERBS 6:20–35

3

Opening Prayer

Scripture Reading

Questions

1 Why should we always listen to our parents' advice? From what will it keep a young man?
2 What are the first two negative admonitions in verses 25–35?
3 What will a prostitute bring a man to?
4 What will an adulteress cost a man?
5 What two illustrations are set forth referring to fire and heat?
6 Does an adulterer suffer a greater penalty than a thief? Why?

NOTE: In Israelite psychology, the adulterer is literally a murderer and worthy of a murderer's fate. Adultery involves the breaking of the marriage contract, hence in ancient Israel, it was more severely punished than any other form of sexual promiscuity; both parties involved were to be put to death by stoning (Deuteronomy 22:22, Ezekiel 18:10–13). It was most degrading to be a harlot, but a harlot was not put to death unless she was an adulteress as well (Leviticus 19:29).

Prayer

CHASTITY AND ADULTERY

THE LOOSE WOMAN—PROVERBS 7:1–27

4

Opening Prayer

Scripture Reading

Questions

1 What familiar admonition is taught in verse 1?
2 What do you think "Say unto wisdom, Thou art my sister" means?

3 What was the young man lacking in verse 7?
4 What do verses 10–12 tell us about the woman?
5 What methods did she employ to get the young man to yield to her? Was she also an adulteress?
6 What are some of the analogies used to show what the man was heading for in verses 22 and 23? Discuss them.
7 What is told to the young man to keep himself pure?

Closing Prayer

CONTROL OF THE TONGUE

THE THOUGHTFUL TONGUE—PROVERBS 10:19

5

Prayer

Scripture Reading

Introduction

The tongue is the most difficult part of our body to control. Chapter three in the Book of James has much to say about the tongue. In verse two, we read, "If anyone can control his tongue, it proves that he has perfect control over himself in every other way." In verse five it says, ". . . the tongue is a small thing, but what enormous damage it can do" (LB). Now let's look to see what Proverbs has to say about the tongue.

Scripture Reading

Questions

1 Turn in your Bibles to Proverbs 10:19; 13:3; 17:28; and 21:23. What do we learn from these verses about being careful of what we say?
2 Now look at Proverbs 15:4, 23; 23:16; 25:15; 31:26 and find out how each of these verses advises us to use the tongue.
3 What does Proverbs 18:21 say about the power of the tongue?

MEMORY VERSE Proverbs 21:23 (optional)

Personal Sharing Time

Have you ever gotten into trouble from saying the wrong thing or by talking too much? How can we stop ourselves from saying the wrong thing when we want very much to say it?

Prayer

Ask the Lord to put a guard on our tongues, that what we say may be pleasing to Him.

CONTROL OF THE TONGUE

PROVERBS 18:6–8, 21

6

Opening Prayer

Scripture

Reading.

Questions

1 Why does the stupid man always get into trouble?
2 Do people like to hear gossip? Do you like to gossip? How can you keep from listening to gossip and evil talk? (*See* Philippians 4:8.)
3 What happens to people who talk too much? Read Proverbs 25:11, 18.
4 What is the comparison regarding "timely advice"? Can you think of a situation where "timely advice" was helpful to you?
5 How strongly does this particular portion of Scripture speak to lying?
6 Read James 3:2–12. In conclusion, what are some of the ways our tongues get us into trouble?

Closing Prayer

CONTROL OF THE TONGUE

LIVING GOD'S WAY—PROVERBS 18–21

7

Prayer

Read Proverbs listed below

Questions

Proverbs 18:4–8—In what ways is our talk an expression of our true selves?

Proverbs 19:17, 23—What blessings come from living God's ways?

Proverbs 20:3, 10, 22, 23, 25—As you read each verse, name those things that are displeasing to the Lord.

Proverbs 21:3, 15, 23, 26, 27, 29—Name characteristics of those who are righteous and wise.

CROSS-REFERENCE *See* James 3:2–13 for further study about speech.

Prayer

Singing

Select a hymn that expresses the desire to follow God and live by His commands.

(Reference Material: *The Christian's Secret of a Happy Life* by Hannah Whitall Smith.)

DILIGENCE AND LAZINESS

PROVERBS 28

8

Opening Prayer

Pray that God will develop godly qualities in each of your lives.

Scripture Reading

This lesson can be divided into two parts using verses 1–14 and 15–28.

This chapter is a list of contrasts. Nearly every verse lists a good quality followed by its opposite bad quality. Teens or adults might find it interesting to list the positive and negative qualities from each verse, and the results of each type of action.

Questions

CHILDREN
1 What is better than being rich and dishonest (verse 6)?
2 What does a wise son do (verse 7)?

(Part 2)
3 Why should we work hard at our chores or schoolwork (verse 19)?
4 How should we act toward the poor (verse 27)?

TEENS
1 How are the wicked and righteous man different in verse 1?
2 When doesn't God hear a person's prayers (verse 9)?

(Part 2) 3 What are the rewards to a person of good character (verses 16, 18, 20)?

4 What is the final position of the wicked and the righteous (verse 28)?

ADULTS 1 What should our attitude be toward the law (verse 4, 5)?

2 What should we do about our faults (verse 13)?

(Part 2) 3 What happens to the grasping person who wants to "get rich quick" (verses 16, 20, 22, 25)?

4 Where should we look for wisdom for living (verse 26)?

What About Me?

What is my attitude toward money? How do I go about earning it? Do I help the poor? How?

What is my attitude toward the law? Toward school rules? Do I support righteous leaders? Do I choose good people as friends to follow?

Springboard (optional)

Many of these verses list not only good and bad qualities, but also the results of these qualities. Look for these verses and discuss life situations where they have been proven true.

Closing Prayer

DILIGENCE AND LAZINESS

LAZINESS—PROVERBS 24:30–34

9

Prayer

Introduction

Proverbs 24:30–34 tells the story of a man who walked by the garden of a lazy person who had allowed the weeds and thorns to ruin it and the walls to fall down. The man learned a valuable lesson from seeing this garden. What do you think it was?

Each of us has jobs that must be done in order to make life run more smoothly for us and those around us. Leaving a job undone will usually cause problems either for ourselves or for the other members of our family. In this case, the gardener was unable to enjoy the delicious fruits and vegetables from a well-cared-for garden. Let us look into the Book of Proverbs for some more lessons on laziness.

Scripture Reading

Questions

1 Turn in your Bibles to Proverbs 6:6–11. From what animal do these verses tell the lazy man to learn? Why? What happens to the person who is lazy?
2 Now turn to Proverbs 10:4, 5; 12:24, 27; 13:4; 15:19. What do these verses say is the difference between the lazy person and the worker?
3 What kind of person is compared with the lazy person in Proverbs 18:9?
4 What do Proverbs 19:15 and 20:4 say will happen to the lazy person?

MEMORY VERSE Proverbs 22:29 LB

Personal Sharing Time

Have you ever left a job undone and been sorry for it later? Did you ever have to spend more time undoing a job that was done poorly than you would have had to spend had you done it carefully the first time?

Prayer

Ask God to make each one a good worker using the time wisely for Him.

DRUNKENNESS AND TEMPERANCE

PROVERBS 23:29–35

10

Prayer

Read Scripture

Questions

1 What does verse 29 mean?
2 What happens when one drinks too much wine?
3 What does verse 35 mean?
4 Read also Proverbs 20:10. Read Proverbs 31:1–9.
5 Whose words are spoken in this chapter? Who taught the prophecy to him?

6 What has King Lemuel's mother done for him (verse 2b)?
7 What does his mother tell him in verse 4? Why?
8 Whom should strong drink be given to? Why?
9 In verses 8 and 9, what does Lemuel's mother advise him to do for certain people? (*Dumb* here refers to those who cannot speak.)
10 Look up 1 Corinthians 6:9, 10.

Prayer

As Paul writes in 1 Corinthians 6:19 (RSV), "Do you not know that your body is a temple of the Holy Spirit within you, which you have from God?" Therefore honor God with your bodies. Please, Lord, help us to do this. In Jesus' Name. *Amen.*

DRUNKENNESS AND TEMPERANCE

OUR ACTIONS BRING CONSEQUENCES—PROVERBS 22:8

11

Prayer

Lord, we ask You to show us in a new way how important it is to live in obedience to Your Word. *Amen.*

Read Scripture

Proverbs 22:8

Questions

Many of the Proverbs tell us how good actions bring about good results and bad actions bring about bad results. What happens to the man who does not act with justice toward others?

Read Proverbs 23:19–21

When people eat too much or drink too much, what is the consequence?

Read Proverbs 22:24, 25

What happens to a person who goes around with the wrong crowd?

Why are our friends important?

Read Proverbs 24:17, 18

How will God feel toward *us* if we are glad when someone we don't like has trouble?

Read Proverbs 24:30–34

What happens to the lazy person who does not do his work?

Have we seen the results of being lazy ourselves?

What are three instructions from the verses we have talked about that we can apply to our own lives right now?

Prayer

Pray that God will help us to *do* His Word and not just hear it.

FRIENDS AND ENEMIES

PROVERBS 27:1–27

12

Prayer

Introduction

Hebrew poetry often used comparison or contrast to present a truth. This chapter lists some things which are better than others. Our lives are always full of choices between the bad, the good, and the best. The second part of the chapter speaks of family relationships and friendships.

Read Scripture

Families with just younger children may read only 1–16. Ask God to help you in practical ways from this passage.

Questions

CHILDREN	1	What is better than praising ourselves (v. 2)?
	2	How should we act toward our friends (v. 10)?
	3	How does a father want his son to act? Why (v. 4)?
TEENS	1	What is worse than anger (v. 4)?
	2	What is better than hidden love (v. 5)?
	3	What is the reward for a well-done job (v. 18)?
ADULTS	1	What should be our attitude toward the future (vs. 1, 12, 23–27)?
	2	What is better than kisses from an enemy (v. 6)?
	3	What is a nagging wife compared to (v. 15)?

What About Me?

Do I brag about myself? How do I feel when others praise themselves? How do I act and feel when others praise me? Do I praise others?

Am I loyal to my friends? How do I treat the friends of others in my family?

Am I a child who brings joy to my parents? Am I a nagging wife? Am I a husband who meets problems wisely?

Springboard (optional)

Encourage each family member to choose one verse from this chapter to memorize.

Make it a practice to praise each other for something every day.

Prayer

Pray that God will bring these thoughts to your mind to help you during the next day.

FRIENDS AND ENEMIES

WITNESSING—PROVERBS 9:7–10

13

Prayer

Introduction

Acts 1:8 says, ". . . ye shall receive power, after that the Holy Ghost is come upon you: and ye shall be witnesses unto me . . . ."

The Christian is asked to ". . . consider how to stir up one another to love and good works" (Hebrews 10:24, 25 RSV) by exhorting or encouraging each other.

Our passage in Proverbs today indicates that when someone tries to help another person know God's ways, he may encounter a strong negative reaction as well as a positive, constructive response for his efforts.

Read Scripture

Questions

1 Compare the reaction of the scoffer or wicked man with that of the wise man when he is corrected or instructed.

2 What goal will encourage the teacher to keep trying (v. 10)?

3 Look now at Proverbs 11:30 and 14:25. What do these verses say about winning souls? Compare these verses with Matthew 9:37, 38 and Matthew 10:32, 33, 38, 39.

Personal Sharing Time

How do you feel about telling your friends about your faith? How do your friends react when they know you feel strongly about your belief in Jesus Christ as your Saviour? Do you feel responsible to God and to your friends to tell them about Him?

Prayer

Thank God for His love for you and ask Him to help you to share that love with those around you.

FRIENDS AND ENEMIES

CHOOSING COMPANIONS—PROVERBS 1, 4, 13, 22, 24

14

Prayer

Introduction

The kind of person you are decides the kind of friend you will make and the friends you make will help to decide what you will become. However, because our heart wants to become friends with a certain person does not necessarily mean that person is best for us. God will give wisdom to those who ask Him for help in selecting the right kind of friends. Let us look at what Proverbs has to say about choosing our friends.

Read Scripture

Questions

1 Read the following verses from Proverbs and name the type of friends God warns against: 1:10; 4:14, 15; 13:20; 22:24, 25; 24:1. How should we avoid the wrong company?
2 Now turn to 16:29 and 22:25. What happens to the person who makes friends with ungodly people?
3 What kind of company does 17:4 say that the wicked and liars choose? How can this apply to you?
4 What does 27:19 say about the friends we choose?

MEMORY VERSE Proverbs 13:20 (optional)

Personal Sharing Time

Share a time when you wanted to do something you knew was wrong just because a friend was doing it.

Prayer

Ask the Lord for wisdom in selecting the right kind of friends.

GOOD OR EVIL

PROVERBS 10–13

15

Prayer

Read Scripture (Living Bible)

We can learn biblical truth by putting it in contrast as some Proverbs do. We see a strong repetition on *one* basic truth in these Proverbs written in contrast. Read them out loud and tell what that truth is.

Questions

YOUNGER CHILDREN Just read certain selections from the list and point out the one truth there.

Proverbs 10: verses 3, 6–9, 11, 20, 21, 28–30, and 32.

Name some characteristics of each group described here.

Proverbs 11: verses 2, 5, 6, 8, 11, 19, 21, 23, 26, and 27.

What are some advantages of goodness?

Proverbs 12: verses 2, 3, 6, 7, 12, 16, 20, 23, and 26.

Proverbs 13: verses 2, 6, 9, 15, 16, 20–22, and 25.

What are some benefits of good living?

MEMORIZE Proverbs 11:27 together. Write it down and post it somewhere obvious to all.

Extra (optional)

What truths can you find in these Proverbs?

1 Proverbs 12:9, 11, 24, 27; 13:4, 11, 14? (Hard work benefits)

2 Proverbs 10:8, 17; 12:1, 8, 15; 13:1, 10, 18. (Open to advice)

Why do you think there is so much repetition in these Proverbs? (The truth taught is of utmost importance in God's eyes.)

Prayer

GOOD OR EVIL

GOD'S WAYS WITH US—PROVERBS 18–21

16

Prayer

Selected Scripture Reading

1 God provides safety for the righteous and is a Friend above all others. Read Proverbs 18:10, 24.

2 God created us, giving us all the physical abilities we have. Read Proverbs 20:12.
3 God is directly involved in the activities of people. Read Proverbs 20:24; and 21:1.
4 God searches our hearts and knows why we do what we do. Read Proverbs 20:27; 21:2.
5 God is all-wise and all-powerful. Read Proverbs 21:30, 31.

Discussion

Choose one of the above portions and talk about how God has dealt with our family.

MEMORIZATION Choose a favorite from the above verses and learn it together.

Prayer

GOOD OR EVIL

GODLINESS AND WICKEDNESS— PROVERBS 6:12–13

17

Opening Prayer

Scripture Reading

Questions

1 What is a wicked man like? How does he show with his body what he is like?
2 What parts of the body are mentioned?
3 How does he spend his time?
4 What will happen to him suddenly?
5 What are the seven things the Lord detests?
6 Why must children obey their parents? What should they do with the teachings of their parents?

Closing Prayer

Psalms 139:1–3, 6–12, 17, 18, 23.

"Search me, O God, and know my heart, try me and know my thoughts: and see if there be any wicked way in me, and lead me in the way everlasting." *Amen.*

GOOD OR EVIL

PROVERBS 10:25, 26; 11:22, 30
(Use Living Bible.)

18

Prayer

Introduction

Proverbs make a picture for us to see in our mind and teach us a truth which we can use, and recall easily. How about these —what do you see?

Read Scripture and Questions

Read Proverbs 10:25. Who are wicked? The good men?

Read Proverbs 10:26. Isn't this a good proverb to remember when looking for work?

Read Proverbs 11:22. Shouldn't a young man consider this when choosing a girl friend?

Read now, Proverbs 11:30. How can you be godly (like God, righteous and loving)?

Discussion

Think over and discuss Proverbs 10:10—how does this apply to you and your family? Is it smart to sweep wrong actions under the rug? Are you this: in discipline? or in business? in a relationship? Maybe there is a need for confessing wrong behavior or attitude toward one another now. This includes parents, too.

Prayer

Take time to pray silently, then have anyone who wishes, pray and share as he wants. Thank God for good relationships among family members, or restored relationships you have mended. Ask Him to help each one see his faults clearly and change so there may be peace and not sorrow.

GOOD OR EVIL

FEAR OF THE LORD—PROVERBS 14:26

19

Prayer

Introduction

We will be reading and discussing the rewards of fearing God but there might be some question as to what this means. Living Bible uses the word *reverence* in the place of fear. It may help to look up the word *reverence* in the dictionary. Proverbs 1:7 says that, "The fear of the Lord is the beginning of knowledge . . . ." Knowledge and understanding lead to trust and obedience.

Scripture Reading

Questions

1 Read verses 26 and 27 chapter 14. Why do you think that a man who fears God would be a man of confidence and strength? What are the benefits to his children?

2 Does verse 27 refer to physical death or eternal death? How can we avoid the snares of death? (*See* 1 Thessalonians 5:22.) What is the promise of this verse (*see* Proverbs 19:23)?

3 Read 15:33. To understand the meaning behind this verse, read Philippians 2:5–11 which tells of Jesus humbling Himself before He received honor and was exalted. Explain, then, in your own words what this verse means.

4 Read Proverbs 16:6. Think about your own Christian experience and state reasons why you would want to be obedient to God and avoid evil (refer, again, to Proverbs 14:16).

5 What is the promise of this verse if we should sin, then turn back to God and remain faithful?

Closing Prayer

Close in prayer and, if you have a Psalter or know any of the Psalms, sing some together.

GUIDELINES FOR FAMILY LIFE

PROVERBS 12, 13

20

Opening Prayer

Introduction

African Elders sit with a group of boys around a burning circle; it is the boys' initiation. It is the first step for them to enter manhood. Many wise words are spoken to teach the boys. It is hard to tell which Elder speaks, but the knowledge of life is set in picture forms—proverbs. The wisdom of war, of farming or cattle, of married life, or the tribe is taught in sayings that are tart and easy to remember. I was once told by a younger African man that he himself was unable to understand the meaning of a conversation by a group of Elders that he had overheard. It was because they were speaking in very ancient proverbs of the tribe known only by the oldest men!

"*Haraka, Haraka, Haina Barake*" (Kiswahili), or as we know it, "Haste makes waste" can stick in the memory well. Sometimes we find parts of the New Testament teaching difficult, as Jesus often taught in parables which are not familiar to the Western mind.

The Book of Proverbs is tested and tried wisdom from God. It is in a frame easy to use in everyday relationships. Here are some to consider and discuss together.

Particular Proverbs for Particular People

Read aloud Proverbs 12:4. Who is this for?

Now try Proverbs 12:25. To which member of the family does this apply?

Read Proverbs 13:13. Isn't this for us all?

What about 13:3? (Check James 3:4–12 also.)

Discussion

SCHOOL-AGE CHILDREN Do you think these sayings could make a difference in your everyday life? See how Proverbs 13:3 can direct you this week at school, and report your experience back to the family.

Last, but not least: for parents. Read Proverbs 13:24. This must be an important point as it is also in Proverbs 3:11, 12 and again in Hebrews 12:5, 6! Do you find yourselves applying Solomon's advice in your own family?

Closing Prayer

Father in Heaven, we each need Your help to start making these teachings a part of us. In Jesus' Name. *Amen.*

GUIDELINES FOR FAMILY LIFE

PROVERBS 18—21

21

Prayer

Scripture Reading

FOR MEN Proverbs 19:14a, 18; 20:7.

FOR WOMEN Proverbs 18:22; 19:13b, 14b; 21:9, 19.

FOR CHILDREN Proverbs 19:13a, 26; 20:11, 20.

Discussion

Honestly talk about how our family lives. Are we treating each other as we should? In what ways can we improve our relationships?

Drama (optional)

Act out an ordinary family situation (doing dishes together, going on a long trip in the car, deciding what TV program to watch, et cetera) and do it with each one acting selfishly. Then do it again, showing how we should act toward each other.

Prayer

(Reference Material: *Love, Honor And . . . ?* by Mary D. Bowman; *Bless This House* by Anita Bryant; *Your Marriage—Duel or Duet?* by Louis H. Evans.)

GUIDELINES FOR FAMILY LIFE

SOME OF GOD'S DIRECTIONS FOR RAISING FAMILIES—PROVERBS 22:6, 15; 23:13–26

22

Prayer

Read Scripture

Use RSV if you have it.

Questions

1 Who has given parents authority over their children?
2 Why does God urge parents to discipline their children?

3 How does the Bible tell mothers and fathers to discipline their children?
4 In addition to using the rod, what other way should a father teach his children?
5 From these verses, how do you think this father feels about his son?
6 What is the goal this father has for his child?
7 What will be the good result if this child learns to obey?

If you have time, use this lesson to lead into a "round table" discussion of the purpose and goals of discipline in your home.

Prayer

Our Dear Heavenly Father, who cares enough for us to discipline us for our good, help us to learn from You the way to give and accept discipline in family life. Help us as parents to be wise and loving in our desire to instruct our children in the ways of obedience. Make our children teachable, we ask, that they might become mature disciples of Your Son, Jesus Christ, our Lord. *Amen.*

GUIDELINES FOR FAMILY LIFE

HEALTH AND LIFE—PROVERBS 14:30

23

Opening Prayer

Introduction

Again the Word of God has much to say about the promise of long life and divine health, but not all of it is covered within these four chapters. We will just touch on this promise in this lesson but other verses will be suggested for your personal study.

Scripture Reading

Questions

1 What is the main ingredient needed for a tranquil mind? (*See* John 12:42; 16:33.)
NOTE: Peace is one thing that Satan cannot imitate. Remember, when there is doubt or confusion, it is not from God. When there is peace in your heart, it is from God.
2 What does peace produce physically and emotionally? What do unrest and envy produce?
3 Read Proverbs 15:4. What do anger and harsh words spoken by the tongue do to our spirits and how does this affect us physically? (*See also* Proverbs 16:24)

4 Read 15:15. Can you think of examples in people's lives (either from Scripture or from personal experience) which point out the truth of this verse?
Should circumstances in our lives make any difference in our attitudes?
How would our attitudes be affected if we applied the command to ". . . give thanks in all circumstances; for this is the will of God in Christ Jesus for you" (1 Thessalonians 5:18 RSV).

5 Read Proverbs 15:30. Reading either King James Version or Revised Standard Version, the first part of this verse reads as follows: "The light of the eyes rejoices the heart" (*see* Luke 11:34 about the light of the eye). How do our inner feelings show forth to others?

6 Read Proverbs 17:22. The conclusion of these verses seems obvious. A happy peaceful heart produces life, but an unhappy, complaining spirit destroys life. Now, how do we go about getting rid of such things as anxiety, anger, worry, hatred, depression et cetera? Think back to the verses that we referred to in this lesson as you answer.

Also read John 10:10; Isaiah 53:5; James 5:15.

Closing Prayer

Since Jesus has come to give us life more abundantly, as you close in prayer if there be any afflictions among you (emotional or physical) come to the Giver of life and seek His healing power.

GUIDELINES FOR FAMILY LIFE

FOOLISHNESS—PROVERBS 14–17

24

Opening Prayer

Open in prayer and ask God for understanding as you study together.

Introduction

Proverbs tells us that foolishness is bound up in the heart of a child and that only the rod of correction will drive it far from him (22:15). If this is not corrected in childhood, it will remain into adulthood. Since this is a family study and this teaching, then, applies to yôung and old, let's take a look at the results of foolishness versus wisdom. Remember, though, it is never too late to ask God to correct something that He brings to light as being wrong within us.

Scripture Reading

Questions

1 Chapter 14:1. What is the result of a foolish woman's mismanagement of a household? What responsibility does this place on the woman of a household?
2 In verse 3, what sin is behind the talk of a foolish man? How can we be rid of pride?
3 What are we to do when given foolish advice (verse 7)?
4 Read verses 8 and 9. How can a foolish man deceive himself into thinking his ways are right? Why do foolish people usually seek the companionship of people like themselves (verse 9)?
5 Read verses 16 and 17. What could be the effects of this type of behavior on neighbors and community? (*See also* 14:29 and 16:29.)
6 What is the reward of the foolish (verse 24)?
7 In chapter 15:5, sons are admonished to listen to their fathers' instructions and suggestions; what responsibility does this place upon the fathers? (*See* verses 2, 7.)
8 In your own words, explain verse 20. (*See* chapter 17:25; you also might want to refer to Ephesians 6:1–3 and Colossians 3:20.)

Closing Prayer

As you close in prayer, a suggestion might be to ask God to reveal any hidden foolishness in your own heart and to take it from you, if you are really willing for it to go.

GUIDELINES FOR FAMILY LIFE

SPARE THE ROD AND SPOIL THE CHILD—SELECTIONS FROM PROVERBS

25

Opening Prayer

Introduction

"Spare the rod and spoil the child." We have heard this old saying so often, that many people probably do not know that the meaning is from the Bible Proverbs. Proverbs has much to say about the discipline of children.

Scripture Reading

Proverbs 13:24; 15:5; 19:18; 22:6, 15; 23:13, 14; 29:15, 17.

Questions

1 What are we told the father who uses the rod shows to his children (13:24)?
2 Why do you feel chastisement is so important in early years (19:18; 22:6)?
3 Do you know of children who are not well disciplined at home? How do they behave? Are they nice to be around?
4 What ways other than the rod can be used to discipline children?
5 Do you feel that spanking or discipline should wait until Father gets home?
6 Read Psalms 127:3. What does it tell you about children and parents?
7 What are we told about children who do not heed their parents' advice (15:5)?
8 What responsibility is given to parents in chapter 23:13, 14? What effects does a child's obedience have upon his parents?

Closing Prayer

GUIDELINES FOR FAMILY LIFE

PROVERBS 31:10–31

26

Opening Prayer

Scripture Reading

Questions

1 What is the value of a good wife (verse 10)? How is her family affected?
2 What does the good wife do for her husband?
3 What type of work does she do in verse 13?
4 What does she do outside of her home?
6 What type of personality does the good wife have? Why?
7 Is she aware of the activities of her family?
8 What are some of her responsibilities in verses 13–23?
9 How is a good wife and mother rewarded in verses 28–31?
10 What type of woman does the Lord say will be honored (vs. 30)?

11 What ways can a Christian mother and wife help in the world today?

Closing Prayer

Eternal God, we thank Thee that Thou didst place us in homes where love is, and parents are. Especially are we grateful for the love of mothers, and we thank Thee for their labors and their prayers and for their faith in us even when we did not deserve it. Help us to so live that our lives may reflect honor upon the names of our mothers and may be worthy of their love.

(Reference: A good book for mothers is *A Mother's Wages* by Elizabeth W. Strachen.)

GUIDELINES FOR FAMILY LIVING

SELECTIONS FROM PROVERBS

27

Opening Prayer

Father, please help us to receive Your Word today with obedient hearts.

Introduction

Today we will look at three short passages concerned with personal behavior. The kind of wisdom that Proverbs deals with touches all of life.

Scripture Reading

Proverbs 6:1–5

Questions

1 (*Surety*—liable for another's debts.) What is the problem here? Would you be willing to share an experience when you made a hasty decision which you regretted afterwards?
2 What are the two choices open to this man? What does his father advise him to do? How does he picture the result if he doesn't?
3 Why is it so hard to say, "I was wrong"?

Read

Proverbs 6:6–11

1 What tiny creature can teach us important lessons? How is it an example to us?
2 Let us not regard work as something to be avoided! Have you ever thought about the fact that work was a part of

God's perfect Creation—even before the Fall? (Read Genesis 2:15.)

Read

Proverbs 4:23–27

1 The word *heart* (verse 23) includes mind, will, and emotion—the very center of one's being. Why is the analogy with a spring a good one?

2 From this passage, what parts of the body may lead one into sin?

3 What can we do to keep our hearts pure? What does God do (1 John 1:9)?

Closing Prayer

Dear Lord, please help us to be more prompt to reject anything that would bring impurity into our hearts. *Amen.*

HONESTY AND LYING

PROVERBS 10–13

28

Opening Prayer

Scripture Reading

Proverbs 11:1, 3; 12:5, 13, 14, 17, 19; 13:5. Memorize one together.

Questions for Younger Children

Do you think God thinks it is important for you to tell the truth—to be honest? How do you know?

Questions for Older Children

Discuss what it means for them to be honest—at home, at school, on their job. Work on memorizing the verse with them.

Honesty or truth, is rare. Even among Christians. God desires truth in the inward part of us. Truth is a characteristic of God. We can best be like Christ by being *loving* and *truthful* (John 14:6).

Closing Prayer

Will you accept the challenge to be true in every area? Ask God to direct you in this now. Maybe He will speak to you as you bow and wait quietly together. Remember the Holy Spirit will lead His own into all Truth.

HONESTY AND LYING

PROVERBS 3:27–35

29

Opening Prayer

Father, we remember that Your Word is given for our instruction and correction, and we thank You for this.

Introduction

The Book of Proverbs has a great deal to say about interpersonal relationships, and the principles involved are as applicable today as they were a few thousand years ago.

Scripture Reading

Questions

1 Let someone give an example of a situation to which verses 27, 28 would apply.

2 Why would anyone "contend" (pick a fight) with someone who had not harmed him? Do you think this verse also applies to children?

3 Violent (wicked) people sometimes seem to prosper and flourish. The psalmist wrestled with this same problem. (*See* Psalm 73:3.) For what reason(s) should we not envy wicked people?

4 Contrast the final outcome of the lives of godly and ungodly people.

5 From this passage, how can you be sure that your good life affects your whole family?

For another passage regarding interpersonal relationships read Proverbs 9:7–9.

1 What kind of a person does not want advice or instruction? Why do you think he reacts like this?

2 How does a wise man react to advice?

3 Take a minute and silently decide what your response is to advice and correction.

4 Have you ever prayed something like this: "O Lord, teach me the way I should go . . . teach me to do Thy will"? Would you be willing for Him to use other people to help teach you?

Closing Prayer

Dear Lord, please help us to be open to receive and to profit from correction and advice. *Amen.*

HONESTY AND LYING

LYING—SELECTIONS FROM PROVERBS

30

Opening Prayer

Introduction

A famous poet once wrote "Oh, what a tangled web we weave when first we practice to deceive." Often when we lie, it has to be defended by a second lie and then a third. In the end, our fear of getting caught becomes more painful than the truth would have been. Adam and Eve ran into many problems for this same reason. Now let's look at what Proverbs has to say about lying.

Scripture Reading and Questions

1 Turn to Proverbs and read the following: 6:16, 17, 19; 12:22. Now compare these verses with Psalms 119:163. How does the psalmist feel about lying?

2 What do Proverbs 12:19 and 14:25 say is the difference between the truth and a lie?

3 Now turn to Proverbs 21:6. What does this verse say about lying?

4 What do Proverbs 19:5, 9 say shall happen to those who (continually) lie?

MEMORY VERSE (optional) Psalms 51:6

Personal Sharing Time

Share a time when you told a lie to get something you wanted very badly or to get out of a punishment that you knew you deserved. How did you feel when the truth was finally known? Why do you think it is important to always tell the truth?

Closing Prayer

Ask God to give you the strength to always be truthful.

RICHES AND POVERTY

HIGHLIGHTING PROVERBS ON VARIOUS TOPICS

31

Opening Prayer

Scripture Reading

Proverbs 14:21, 31, and 17:5

Questions

1 What would your attitude be towards a poor friend or neighbor? What should our attitude be? Read what Jesus says about our attitude towards the less fortunate (Matthew 25:31–40).

2 Read Proverbs 14:34. What nation in the Old Testament experienced the effects of sin many times?
How does this verse relate to our own nation today?

3 Read 15:27. What does this say to you concerning your own family's financial dealings? For example, figuring your income tax forms? Consider the results of disobedience.

4 Read 15:29. Many people complain that God does not answer prayer. According to this verse, why is this so? (*See* Isaiah 59:2.)

5 Read Proverbs 16:3. This verse has special meaning to me as it is the promise I am claiming as I do these lessons. What does this mean to you either in your job as a housewife, student, or wage earner?

6 Read 17:13. What kind of household would this be? What effect would this have upon the children, even into the next generations? (*See* Exodus 20:5 and 34:7.)

Closing Prayer

Conclude with a prayer of praise to God for each other and for a home which is centered on and interested in His Word. Also, ask the Holy Spirit to bring someone to mind who is in need and ask the Lord what you might do to help him: God bless you. *Amen.*

RICHES AND POVERTY

HOW GOD REGARDS THE POOR—PROVERBS 22

32

Prayer

Dear Heavenly Father, please give us Your perspective about the many material blessings You have given us. Help us to see our thoughts and motives and attitudes the way You see them. Give us a desire to be Your servants in the lives of those around us that they might come to know Your Son, Jesus Christ, as the Lord and Saviour of their lives. *Amen.*

Read Scripture

Proverbs 22:2, 7–9, 22, 23

Questions

1 Who has made both the rich and poor?
2 What kind of power can a rich man have over a poor one?
3 What would be a wrong use of that power?
4 How can a rich man use his power for the Lord?
5 What man does God bless (22:9)?
6 What will happen to the man who oppresses the poor to increase his own wealth?
7 Who pleads the cause of the poor, the afflicted, and the fatherless?
8 What will God do to those who harm the poor?
9 Who are the poor around us?
10 What are some things a family can do to help them?
11 What is one thing we could do ourselves?

Prayer

Pray that God would show your family some specific way to help someone else who is in need.

RICHES AND POVERTY

THE SEEING EYE—SELECTIONS FROM PROVERBS

33

Prayer

Someone once stated that "the eyes are the windows of our soul." In Luke 11:34 LB we read, "Your eyes light up your inward being. A pure eye lets sunshine into your soul." (Sing or read the chorus of "Turn Your Eyes Upon Jesus.")

Read Scripture

Questions

Let's look now into the Book of Proverbs to see what is written there about our eyes.

1 Turn in your Bibles to Proverbs 5:21 and 15:3. What do these verses say about the eyes of God?
2 Now look at Proverbs 22:9. What kind of an eye does God bless?
3 Proverbs 28:27 tells us what will happen to those who refuse to see the needs of those around them. How can we as a family be more aware of the needs of others? Is there anyone we know who needs our help? What shall we do for them?

4 Turn now to Proverbs 23:5 and 28:22. When we "set our eyes upon" something it means that we make that thing our goal. What goal does God warn about? Why shouldn't we make money our goal? What kind of poverty might come upon a person who makes riches his goal? What are some good goals for this family to set our eyes upon?

Prayer

Ask God to help us to give our eyes to Him that we may see what He wants us to see.

RICHES AND POVERTY

WEALTH—SELECTIONS FROM PROVERBS

34

Prayer

Pray that your family will be open to what God would teach through this portion of Scripture.

Read Scripture

Proverbs 22:1, 2 and 23:4, 5

Questions

Is it an important thing in God's sight to be rich?

Does a rich man mean more to God than a poor man?

What does God say is more important than riches? Than silver or gold?

Many places in the Bible God tells us how important it is to work hard and to do our work well. In Ephesians 6:5–9, God tells us that people should do their very best work to please Him. But in Proverbs 23:4, God tells us there is something we should *not* work hard for. What is it?

Why does God warn us not to work hard to get rich?

Read Scripture

Proverbs 22:4

This is a case where God makes riches a reward. Who is rewarded with riches?

Do you think that a person who is full of humility and respect for the Lord would use his riches the wrong way?

Taking all of these verses together, what do they show about how God regards riches?

What Can We Learn?

1 The most important thing in life is our heart's attitude toward God the Father, Son, and Holy Spirit.

2 When riches are the main goal of life, they bring much unhappiness.
3 Riches rightly used can be a blessing in the lives of others.

Prayer

Dear Lord Jesus Christ, please keep us seeking after You each day instead of the temporary riches the world has to offer. *Amen.*

SELF-CONTROL

ANGER—SELECTIONS FROM PROVERBS

35

Prayer

Introduction

Anger is one of man's strongest feelings. Many great men in the Bible have sinned because of their anger, and God has included many verses in the Bible about it. It is a feeling that is hard to control, and is harmful both to the angry person and to those with whom he is angry. Let's look at the Book of Proverbs to see what God has there about anger.

Scripture Reading

Questions

1 Turn in your Bibles to Proverbs 14:17; 15:18; 19:19; and 29:20, 22. What do these verses say about an angry person?
2 How does Proverbs 22:24, 25 say we should treat an angry person?
3 Now turn to Proverbs 14:29, 15:1; 16:32; 17:27; and 29:8. How does the wise man deal with anger?

MEMORY VERSE Proverbs 16:32 (optional)

Personal Sharing Time

Discuss times when you have become angry and lost your temper. How did you feel when it was over? Share times when you have controlled your temper and tell how you felt about it.

Prayer

Ask God to help you to control your anger. Ask Him to fill your heart with His love instead.

SELF-CONTROL

PROVERBS 29

36

Prayer

Scripture Reading

Read Proverbs 29, or do this lesson in two parts using verses 1–11 and 12–27. Pray that God will convict of sin in your lives where necessary, and lead you in right living.

Again the writer of Proverbs uses contrast. In verses 1–11, he shows the differences between the wicked man and the righteous man. God's plans for good government are revealed. There are also instructions to sons, and general rules for living.

Questions

CHILDREN	1	How does a father feel about a wise son (v. 3)?
	2	Do the wise or the foolish start fights (v. 8)?
(Part 2)	3	Why do my parents punish me when I've done something wrong (vs. 15, 17)?
	4	What is the result of trusting in God (v. 25)?
TEENS	1	What happens if we refuse to accept criticism (v. 1)?
	2	How does a wise man handle his anger (v. 11)?
(Part 2)	3	What happens when people live as if there is no God (v. 18)?
	4	What are the results of pride? of humility (v. 23)?
ADULTS	1	Read verse 4 again. Why is this true?
	2	How can flattery be a trap (v. 5)?
(Part 2)	3	How can verse 19 be applied to an employer-employee relationship?
	4	Can verse 21 be applied to raising children? How?

What About Me?

Do I exhibit the characteristics of the wicked—stubborn (v. 1), wasteful (v. 3), caught in sin (v. 6), arrogant (v. 8), angry (v. 11)? Or, do I exhibit the characteristics of the righteous—bringing joy to my parents (v. 3), showing concern for the helpless (v. 7), wise (v. 7), controlling my anger (v. 11)?

For children—How do I respond when my parents punish me?

For parents—Do I punish my children for the correct reasons?

Springboard (optional)

This might be a good time to discuss the behavior that is not acceptable in your family and to decide together on appropriate and fair disciplines.

Prayer

Pray that God will increase the love and sense of unity in your family.

WISDOM AND COMMON SENSE

GOD URGES US TO GET WISDOM— SELECTIONS FROM PROVERBS

(For young children)

37

Prayer

Read Scripture

Proverbs 22:17–21. Use of the Living Bible is suggested.

1 How do we learn about God?
2 Why should we learn about God (v. 19)?
3 What does learning about God do for us?

Proverbs 24:13, 14, 21, 22

4 When you eat honey, does it taste good?
5 What words would you use to tell about how honey tastes?
6 What does Solomon tell us in these verses is like eating honey?
7 What is wisdom?

Proverbs 25:11, 12

In these verses, God tells us that it is a very beautiful thing to be able to listen carefully and learn when someone tells us what we should do.

8 What word picture does Solomon use to tell us about good advice?
9 Can you make your own word picture?
10 Do you think a truly wise person is one who knows a lot, or one who does what he knows God wants him to do?

Prayer

Ask God to make you the best kind of wise person—one who knows what God wants and does it.

WISDOM AND COMMON SENSE

GODLINESS TAUGHT TO YOUTH— PROVERBS 1:1–9

38

Prayer

Scripture Reading

Questions

1 Who is King Solomon?
2 What is the purpose of the Proverbs (verses 2–4)?
3 What is a proverb?
4 What happens to the simple-minded people as a result of listening to the Proverb? to the young people? to the wise?
5 What type of person refuses to be taught (v. 7)?
6 Do you feel wisdom is hard won?
7 Do you have to be wise to be really godly (v. 7)?
8 In verse 8, what instructions are given to children regarding their parents?
9 In verse 7, what does the fear of the Lord mean to you? (*Fear* here is the fear coming from love, the fear of displeasing the Lord.)

Prayer or Benediction

WISDOM AND COMMON SENSE

PROVERBS 26:1–22

39

Prayer

Read Scripture

If there are only young children in your family, you may limit the reading to verses 1–6 and 13–22. Pray that God will give His wisdom to each of you.

We meet some very undesirable friends in this passage . . . the stupid man, the lazy man, and the troublemaker. Sometimes we act like these men ourselves. But, as Christians, Christ lives in us, and we can be wise, productive, and peaceful.

Questions

CHILDREN
1 How must a stupid man be guided (v. 3)?
2 What kind of person starts fights easily (v. 21)?
3 What will a person who wants to fight do (v. 21)?

TEENS
1 What is lacking in a stupid man (v. 1)?
2 Why shouldn't we engage in senseless arguments (v. 4)?
3 What excuse does the lazy man give for not working (v. 13)?
4 What happens if we try to cover up a lie (v. 18, 19)?

ADULTS
1 What effect do wise sayings have on the stupid man (v. 7, 9)?
2 What are the employment prospects of the unwise man (v. 6, 10)?
3 What characteristic do the stupid man and the sluggard share (vs. 12, 16)?
4 What do verses 20 and 22 say about gossip?

What About Me?

Am I like the unwise man? Can I be trusted with a job? Do I make excuses for not getting a job done? Do I listen to good advice? Do I repeat my mistakes?

Am I like the lazy man? Do I have trouble getting out of bed in the morning? If so, why?

Do I lie and then try to cover it up? Do I start fights? Am I a gossip?

Springboard (optional)

Discuss verse 17. Should we come to the aid of someone engaged in a quarrel? Why not? Or, if so, when?

Go through the passage again and notice all the times the natural world and animals are used to explain the truths.

Prayer

Pray that God will strengthen each of you to be wise, productive, and peace-loving.

WISDOM AND COMMON SENSE

WISDOM—PROVERBS 3:21–26
(Teens)

40

Opening Prayer

Father, we believe with all our hearts the words of Christ that man shall not live by bread alone, but by every word that comes from the mouth of God.

Introduction

Remembering that wisdom is "the right use of knowledge," we move on to other passages in this book in which a father pleads with his son to give careful attention to the importance of wisdom in his life.

Scripture Reading

Questions

1 Against what danger does the father warn in verse 21?
2 What will characterize the life of a person who "keeps sound wisdom"?
3 What are some of the ways the non-Christian tries to build security into life? What is God's way?
4 "Freedom from Fear" was one of Franklin D. Roosevelt's utopian Four Freedoms. How does Solomon see that this may be attained?
5 Can you think specifically how knowing God (Proverbs 2:5) releases us from fears? Do you have any recurring fear? Is it anything an all-wise, all-powerful, loving Heavenly Father cannot handle? The best antidote to fear is always thoughtful meditation about the One who is our Keeper (v. 26).
6 What is the one kind of fear that is good and desirable? Read Proverbs 2:5 and 1:7. What does this mean? (Having wisdom apparently depends on understanding this. "The fear of the Lord is the beginning of knowledge.")

NOTE: A profitable quarter-hour could be spent with a concordance (at some other time) looking up references that speak about "the fear of God" (optional).

Closing Prayer

We thank You, dear Lord, that we are always in the care of a loving Heavenly Father. *Amen.*

WISDOM AND COMMON SENSE

PROVERBS 4:1–7
(Teens)

41

Opening Prayer

Father, please help us to be doers of the Word, and not hearers only.

Parents since Solomon's day (and before!) have tried to advise their children about the right way to live.

Scripture Reading

Proverbs 4:1–7

Questions

1 The father said, "Hear," "Listen to me." Compare Luke 8:18 for Christ's words about hearing.

2 What should parents keep in mind when they are advising their young people? What should the young people keep in mind?

3 Read 1 Chronicles 28:9 to see how Solomon's father advised him.

4 "Get wisdom, and whatever you get, get insight" (RSV). Is this the usual fatherly advice in twentieth century America? What are some of the contemporary goals held before the eyes of young people?

Read

Proverbs 8:14–31

Wisdom is personified in this passage, speaking in the first person.

1 Make a list of the benefits she promises.

2 What word in verse 18 gives you the clue that she is not speaking about material riches and prosperity? What other kind is there?

3 Verses 22–31 give a flashback to pre-Creation "time." Wisdom says she was there. Of course! All wisdom flows from the eternal God, who is all-wise. What specific acts of Creation does Wisdom mention?

4 Let each member of the family suggest one example of God's wisdom in His Creation.

Closing Prayer

Dear Lord, Your Creation shows us Your power and Your wisdom. How great Thou art! *Amen.*

WISDOM AND COMMON SENSE

FEET—SELECTIONS FROM PROVERBS

(Use King James Version or Revised Standard Version.)

42

Opening Prayer

Introduction

Psalms 37:23 says "The steps of a good man are ordered by the Lord: and he delighteth in his way." The Christian is often compared to a pilgrim on a journey from earth to heaven. God has given us the Bible to use as a map to show us the way. If the Lord Jesus guides each step we take, and if we call upon Him when the path becomes rough or we become unsure of our footing, the journey will be a joyful one. Let's look into the Book of Proverbs for some guidelines for our feet.

Scripture Reading and Questions

1 Turn in your Bibles to Proverbs 3:21. What instructions should we follow in order to get the blessings in verses 3:23, 26?

2 Now turn to Proverbs 4:26, 27. What four things do these verses warn us to do?

3 Proverbs 6:18 tells us of a kind of foot that the Lord hates. What is it?

4 What things do the following verses, Proverbs 10:9; 13:20, say about our walk?

MEMORY VERSE Psalms 119:59 (optional)

Personal Sharing Time

Name some places where you go that you know are pleasing to the Lord. Are there more places like these that you should be going to but aren't?

Closing Prayer

Ask God to guide each step you take.

WISDOM AND COMMON SENSE

THE LISTENING EAR—SELECTIONS FROM PROVERBS

43

Opening Prayer

Introduction

We can only follow instructions if we listen carefully to them. Sounds passing through the chambers of our ear touch nerves which take messages to our brain. It is not until our brain receives the message that we have heard. It is through the careful use of our ears that we receive the instructions of God, our parents, and our teachers. Let's look at the Book of Proverbs to see what God says about our ears.

Scripture Reading and Questions

1 Turn in your Bibles to Proverbs 20:12. Who made our listening ear?

2 Look now at Proverbs 22:17 and 23:12. What does God command us to do with our ears?

3 Now turn to Proverbs 1:8; 4:1; 6:20. Whose instructions does God ask us to hear? Why do you think this is important?

4 What blessings do Proverbs 1:5; 1:33; 4:10; and 8:32, 33 tell us we can receive when we listen to God?

Personal Sharing Time

Discuss the times when you failed to listen to instructions and ran into trouble. Discuss other ways in which failing to listen can harm you or cause you problems.

Closing Prayer

Ask God to help us to listen carefully to the instructions of those who love us.

WISDOM AND COMMON SENSE

THE WISE AND UNDERSTANDING HEART—SELECTIONS FROM PROVERBS

44

Opening Prayer

Introduction

In Proverbs 4:23 (NEB), we read, "Guard your heart more than any treasure, for it is the source of all life." Just as our physical heart sends the blood which keeps us alive to all parts of our bodies, so our spiritual heart sends all information that we receive—both good and bad—into the way we live. There is a lovely old hymn that goes:

"Give me thy heart, give me thy heart"
Hear the soft whisper, wherever thou art;
From this dark world He would draw thee apart
Speaking so tenderly, "Give me thy heart."

Scripture Reading

Let's look now to see what the Book of Proverbs says about our hearts.

Questions

1 Read the following verses from Proverbs: 2:2; 14:33; 22:17; 23:12, 15. When Solomon became King of Israel, God promised to grant him one wish. King Solomon asked for wisdom which he valued above all else. Proverbs has much to say about the wise and understanding heart. What do you think it means to have such a heart? How is it possible to have one?

2 Turn now to Proverbs 3:1; 4:4; and 6:21. Compare these verses with Psalms 119:11. How can we be sure to remember God's Word?

3 What do these following verses say about our hearts? Proverbs 3:5, 6; 16:9; 28:14.

MEMORY VERSE Proverbs 23:26 (optional)

Personal Sharing Time

How does each of our hearts look to God? Have all of us given ourselves to God to make us what He wants us to be?

Closing Prayer

Ask God to cleanse our hearts and fill us with Himself and with His wisdom and understanding.

WISDOM AND COMMON SENSE

PROVERBS 30

45

Opening Prayer

Pray that God will teach you the meaning of humility as revealed in His Word.

Introduction

This chapter contains the proverbs of a man named Agur. We know only his name, but what he writes tells us about the kind of person he was. Verses 1–14 describe the humble man and his attitudes. The second part of this chapter could be called Agur's "Book of Records." He lists five groups of things which share a common extreme characteristic. He tells the things which are not able to be satisfied, the most wonderful, the most earth-shaking, the smallest yet wisest, and the stateliest.

Scripture Reading

Proverbs 30, or in two parts using verses 1–14 and verses 15–33.

Questions

CHILDREN
1 What does the writer say about God's Word (verse 5)?
2 For what two things does the writer ask God (verses 7, 8)?
(Part 2) 3 Why are the ants described as wise (verse 25)?
4 What causes fights (verse 33)?

TEENS
1 What are the answers to the questions asked in verse 4?
2 How does the writer describe those who curse their parents (verses 11–14)?
(Part 2) 3 What four things does the writer say are too wonderful for him to understand (verses 18, 19)?
4 What four things are smallest, yet wisest (verses 24–28)?

ADULTS
1 How does the writer describe himself in verses 1–3?

2 Why does the writer ask to be neither poor nor rich (verses 7–9)?

(Part 2) 3 What four things are classified as earth-shaking (verses 21–23)?

4 Explain the four things which are never satisfied (verses 15, 16).

What About Me?

Do I believe God's words are true? Is He my defender?

How do I feel about what I have? Do I have enough money? toys? big enough house? enough clothes?

Springboard (optional)

Notice the many references to the natural world and animals in this passage. What animals are mentioned? Why are they singled out?

Try to compose a list such as we find in this chapter. Your list could be of things which are strong, yet gentle; most beautiful; or most peaceful, and so forth.

Closing Prayer

Make your closing prayer a time of thanks—for the truth of God's Word and for the blessings He has given each of you.

WISDOM AND COMMON SENSE

WISDOM—SELECTIONS FROM PROVERBS

46

Opening Prayer

Scripture Reading and Questions

1 What is wisdom? (*See* chapter 2 of Proverbs)
2 Who is the source of wisdom?
3 Read chapter 14 verse 6. Why does the one who scorns or mocks God try to find wisdom and not receive it? Where is he looking?
4 Read 16:20–23. What are some of the benefits or blessings found in these verses as the result of using wisdom?
5 Give examples of how these principles could help a Christian to witness to others about Jesus Christ.
6 Read 17:16. In other words, would it be wise to pay to educate a child who had no desire to learn?
7 Read 17:24. Does this mean that all who seek wisdom may receive it? Remember chapter 2.

Drama Suggestion (optional)

Depending on the makeup of your family, a fun thing to do with some of these lessons in Proverbs might be to participate in a little drama. One might take the part of the foolish, for example, and another the part of the wise. Choose the verses that appeal to you most for this type of thing. Think of situations that characterize the situations mentioned and don't worry about going to extremes. Remember, that very often in life people do go to extremes in their behavior. Have fun!

Closing Prayer

If you have decided after studying God's Word that you may ask Him for the gift of wisdom, as you close in prayer consider this request.

WISDOM AND COMMON SENSE

THE KNOWLEDGE OF GOD—PROVERBS 3:1–18

47

Opening Prayer

Scripture Reading

Questions

1 What will you receive if you do not forget the teaching in verses 1 and 2?
2 What things come from being truthful? Can you think of any instances when being truthful has hurt you?
3 What does verse 5 mean to you? Did you do that today? What happened?
4 What happens if you put God first in your life?
5 What should be done with the money you earn?
6 Why should we not resent being corrected by the Lord?
7 Does wealth bring happiness?
8 What five things does wisdom bring (vs. 16, 17)?

Closing Prayer Suggestion

Our Shepherd knows what pastures are best for His sheep and we must not question or doubt, but trustingly follow Him. Help us to learn to do this, Lord. In Jesus' Name, *Amen.*

WISDOM AND COMMON SENSE

WISDOM—PROVERBS 2:1–20
(Teens)

48

Opening Prayer

Father, we pray that the Holy Spirit will apply the Word to our own lives today.

Scripture Reading

Proverbs 3:13–15

King Solomon, who had absolutely everything (1 Kings 10:23) —and who should have known!—advises his son that the most desirable thing in all the world is wisdom.

Questions

Proverbs 2:1–20

1 Though *wisdom* is not clearly defined in this passage, what words help describe it?
2 Look up meanings in a dictionary and see what is the difference between *knowledge* and *wisdom.*
3 How do you like this definition of wisdom: "Wisdom is a right use of knowledge." Could you think of a better one?
4 How do you know from this passage that Solomon is not talking about just human wisdom?
5 What are the conditions for receiving this kind of wisdom?
6 Even beyond wisdom itself, what is the highest good that comes to one who meets these conditions? (*See* verse 5 and Proverbs 9:10.)
7 We may pray for wisdom, or to know God better (verse 3), but verse 4 tells us this also requires some effort on our part. Specifically, what do you think we can do to attain these goals?
8 List the benefits of attaining this kind of wisdom and understanding of God.

Closing Prayer

Dear Lord, we thank You with all our hearts that You have made it possible for us to know You through Christ. We pray to know You better. *Amen.*

(For older readers: One of the finest books about how to know God better is *Knowledge of the Holy* by A. W. Tozer. It is highly recommended.)

OPEN-BOOK QUIZ

OUR CHOICE—WHAT KINDS OF PERSONS DO WE WANT TO BE?—SELECTIONS FROM PROVERBS 18–21

49

Prayer

Scripture Reading

Read some or all of the following verses. After a verse is read, match one or more characteristics from the list below.

Proverbs 18:1, 9, 12, 13, 15, 17.
Proverbs 19:2, 3, 8, 11, 15, 20, 22, 24, 28.
Proverbs 20:4, 6, 13, 15, 17.
Proverbs 21:4, 6, 24, 25, 26, 28.

Dishonest	Honest	Kind	Stingy
Faithful	Humble	Lazy	Truthful
Foolish	Ignorant	Peace loving	Untruthful
Generous	Industrious	Proud	Untrustworthy
Hasty	Just	Sinful	Wise

CROSS-REFERENCE Galatians 5:19–23

Prayer

Ask God to help us be the kinds of persons He wants us to be.

OPEN-BOOK QUIZ

CONSEQUENCES OF SIN—SELECTIONS FROM PROVERBS 18–21

50

Prayer

Scripture Reading

Proverbs 18:12, 19, 21.
Proverbs 19:5, 9, 16, 19, 29.
Proverbs 20:17, 20, 21, 26, 30.
Proverbs 21:7, 12, 13, 15, 16, 18, 28, 29.

True or False

1 Pride leads to honor and humility leads to destruction.
2 It is very difficult to win back a friend who has been offended.

3 One can say whatever one likes and suffer no consequences.
4 Disobedience to God's Commandments leads to death.
5 Those who enjoy cheating will find it leaves a pleasant taste in their mouths.
6 Punishment helps to turn people from wrongdoing.
7 God will bring judgment upon those who will not turn from their wicked ways.
8 Neglecting to help the poor is not an offense.

CROSS-REFERENCES Romans 6:23, 1 Peter 2:24; 3:18, 1 John 1:9.

Prayer

OPEN-BOOK QUIZ

PROVERBS 10–13
(Use Living Bible.)

51

Prayer

Since these Bible Proverbs can help us live in a better way with our family and friends, enable us to learn and use them often, Lord. *Amen.*

Read Scripture

Questions

Who wrote most of the Proverbs (10:1)?
Can you give several examples of a two-line Proverb (10–13)?
What themes do you see repeated? (Honesty vs. Lying; Hard Work vs. Laziness; Godly vs. Wicked)

True or False

_____ It is possible to give away and become richer! It is also possible to hold on too tightly and lose everything (Proverbs 11:24, 25).
_____ The wicked shall stand; the godly shall perish (Proverbs 12:7).
_____ God loves those who keep their promises and hates those who don't (Proverbs 12:22).
_____ Pride leads to a fall; be humble, take advice and become wise (Proverbs 13:10).

Fill In

1 The Lord's blessing is our greatest _________ (Proverbs 10:22). All our work adds _________ to it!
2 Reverence for God adds _________ to each day (Proverbs 10:27). So how can the _________ expect a long, good life?

3 Happy is the man with a ________ son; sad the mother of a ________ (Proverbs 10:1).
4 Winking at sin leads to ________ (Proverbs 10:10). Bold reproof leads to ________.
5 Lies will get any man into ________ (Proverbs 12:13) but ________ is its own defense.
6 Work harder and become a ________ (Proverbs 12:24). Be ________ and never succeed.
7 Be with ________ and become ________ (Proverbs 13:20). Be with ________ and become ________.
8 God protects the ________ but destroys the ________ (Proverbs 10:29).

Matching Proverbs

Love	11:17
Gossip	10:19
Hope	10:5
Self-control	12:13
Ambition	10:28
Honesty	10:12
Kindness	11:13

PALESTINE

APPROXIMATE SCALE

Studies in John

It is almost universally agreed that the writer of the fourth Gospel was John, the son of Zebedee, and brother of James. He possibly was a first cousin of Jesus through his mother, Salome, Mary's sister. John and James were called Sons of Thunder (*see* Mark 3:17) because they were so fiery and impetuous. However, John is also known as the Beloved Disciple. It was he who leaned on Jesus' bosom at the Last Supper; who stood faithful at the cross and was entrusted with the care of Jesus' mother. He was one of the first of the apostles to recognize Jesus' Resurrection and the first to perceive the Lord at the lake shore. All of these events are recorded in this Gospel, but others also put John in the inner circle close to Jesus. (*See* Mark 5:37; Luke 8:51; Matthew 17:1.)

It is believed that the Gospel of John was written about A.D. 90 to counteract the false teachings that grew up during the first century of Christianity's growth. Not unlike some of today's false teachings, they blended philosophy, oriental religions, and Christianity. The apostle's reasons for setting down what he had seen Jesus do and what he had heard Him say are best stated in John's own words: "But these are written, that ye might believe that Jesus is the Christ, the Son of God; and that believing ye might have life through his name" (John 20:31 KJV).

John differs from the other Gospels. Most of the content of John is unique, whereas Matthew, Mark, and Luke contain much of the same material presented differently. He does not touch on Jesus' earthly beginnings at all, but instead gives us Jesus' heavenly origin with God, His coming into the world, and what this means to the world. His firsthand knowledge of the miracles and teaching of Jesus emphasizes over and over again that He was God dwelling among us (1:14).

The Book of John is a favorite of many people because of the thread of love running through it: God's love for man. Perhaps John 3:16 says it best: "For God so loved the world, that he gave his only begotten Son, that whosoever believeth in him should not perish, but have everlasting life." All mankind has a need for love and forgiveness of sin. The story of the Bible is the glorious revelation of God and His ways. It shows the Creator reaching out to man whom He created in love and mercy. No Book presents this truth more clearly than John. John's message to the Christians of his day applies just as much to us in the twentieth century when men would water down Christianity. Here is God the Son coming to His own Creation, ". . . not to condemn the world, but that the world might be saved through him" (John 3:17 RSV). Some of the passages may be difficult for young children to understand, but *love* is a concept familiar to even your youngest child. As you study John's Gospel with your family, pray that the Holy Spirit will reveal this Book of love to you all.

(NOTE: Some lessons are marked *A* for alternate. These present a different aspect of the same passages. For greater understanding, you may want to do both lessons.)

PROLOGUE TO THE BOOK OF JOHN—JOHN 1:1–18

(The Revised Standard Version is used in this study.)

1

Introduction

As most people know, the Gospel of John contains accounts from the life of Christ. But quite in contrast, instead of starting with genealogies and details surrounding His birth in Bethlehem (as Matthew and Luke did), or instead of opening with the beginning of Jesus' public ministry (as Mark did), John chose to introduce his account with a beautiful, poetical *Prologue*, which stands serene as a majestic hymn to the Word of God. It is best understood when seen in the light of John's stated purpose in writing (John 20:31). He wanted the readers to believe that Jesus is the Christ, God's Son, and to obtain life by believing in His name.

These first eighteen verses of John are a summary of everything that follows from the nineteenth verse of chapter 1 to the twenty-ninth verse of chapter 20.

Prayer

Open with prayer, asking for wisdom to understand the poetic language of these verses.

Read Scripture

John 1:1–18

Questions

1 John 1:1 Who is the Word? This is one of the names of Jesus. Revelation 19:13 states, ". . . the name by which he is called is The Word of God." What an appropriate name for Christ, since God chose to reveal Himself more fully through Christ.

2 When did Christ begin to exist? We gain further understanding into this question in John 17:5 when Christ refers to the glory He had with God before the world was made.

3 Who is Christ according to verse 1?

4 John 1:3 How was Christ involved with Creation? In Genesis 1:26, we read "Then God said, 'Let *us* make man in our image. . . .' "

5 Reread John 1:4. What does this verse mean? Could it be explained this way: Christ is the source of all life and only in Christ does life have meaning?
In John 8:12, Christ said, ". . . I am the light of the world; he who follows me will not walk in darkness, but will have the light of life."

6 John 1:5 What does darkness refer to in this verse? You may gain further understanding of this thought from the following verses: John 3:19–21; Acts 26:18; and 1 John 1:5–7.

7 John 1:6–8 Who is this man John?

8 What was John's purpose in life?

9 John 1:9 Who is the true light?

10 John 1:10, 11 Did the people of Christ's day recognize Him for who He was?

11 John 1:12, 13 What happens to all who do recognize Him for who He was?

12 John 1:14 What day on our calendar does this verse bring to mind?

13 John 1:18 Who is the only person who has ever seen God?

Food for Thought

1 The words "In the beginning . . . ." of John 1:1 remind us of the very first words in the Bible in Genesis 1:1, "In the beginning God created the heavens and the earth." Christ was there in Genesis 1:1! Let your mind rest on that thought a moment. How has the fact of John 1:14, "The

Word became flesh and dwelt among us . . . ," affected your life?

2 How does one become a child of God? Explain what the words "received him" mean in John 1:12.

3 Can we learn anything from John the Baptist about witnessing for Christ?

Closing

Close with a prayer of thanksgiving.

(Reference: *The Gospel According to John* by G. Campbell Morgan, pages 18–19.)

JOHN 1:19–29

2

Prayer

Introduction

John the Baptist was a man sent from God (John 1:6) to prepare the way of the Lord (Matthew 3:3). He was predicted in the Old Testament (Isaiah 40) and even his birth was a miracle. He knew his place was to bring honor to the Lord Jesus.

Read Scripture

Questions

1 Turn in your Bibles to John 1:19–23.
   - a Who did the Jews from Jerusalem send to question John?
   - b What questions did they ask him?
   - c What were his answers?
   - d What was John's whole purpose in life?

2 Now read verses 24–27.
   - a From what group were those that questioned John the Baptist?
   - b What did they ask him in verse 25?
   - c What was his answer (v. 26)?
   - d Of whom was John the Baptist speaking in verses 25, 26?

3 Read verses 28 and 29.
   - a What was John doing when these people came to see him?
   - b Who else came to see John the Baptist?
   - c What did John say to Him?

Personal Sharing Time

John identified with Jesus, was not ashamed to stand up for Him, and let the world know that he was on earth to glorify the Lord. How does our life measure up to John's?

As John prepared the way for the coming of Christ and gave witness of Him to the people of his day, how might we prepare the way for the coming of Christ to those who don't know Him?

Prayer

Thank Jesus for His wonderful plan for our salvation and ask Him to help us to be a witness to those around us that Jesus is coming again.

WITNESSING—JOHN 1:29–45

3

Prayer by the leader

Our Father, as we read Thy Word together may we understand the truth written there, and may we live and work together as a family, united in Thy love, strengthened by Thy power, and guided by Thy wisdom. Help us to do all things for Thy glory. *Amen.*

Read Scripture

Questions

CHILDREN	What did John call Jesus? Who did Andrew tell about Jesus?
TEEN-AGERS	As the Lamb of God, what would Jesus do for the world? Why did God send the sign of a dove at the baptism of Jesus?
ADULTS	Describe the chain of witness portrayed in this passage. What indication is there that the disciples were familiar with Old Testament prophecies concerning Jesus?

Discuss

Can you find all the names given Jesus? (Lamb of God; Son of God; Rabbi; Messiah, the Christ; Jesus of Nazareth; son of Joseph.) Discuss how Jesus fulfills the meaning of each name.

Drama (optional)

What are some of the ways we can invite others to follow Jesus? Act out one of them.

Prayer

Ask the family for special requests.

(Reference: *Portraits of Christ* by Henry Gariepy.)

THE MARRIAGE AT CANA—JOHN 2:1–12

4

Prayer

Introduction

Although archaeologists are not sure of the location of this little town called Cana, everyone agrees that it was nestled up in the hill country of Galilee. In order to get to the nearby big town, you had to go "down" to Capernaum, by the Sea of Galilee (2:12).

Read Scripture

Questions

1 What happy thing was going on? List the different people who had been invited. To find the five disciples who came with Jesus see 1:37–42. Cana was Nathanael's home town (21:2).

2 What serious problem arose? Who was sensitive to the need? Why was she qualified to suggest a solution (Luke 1:28–33)?

When Jesus called His mother "Woman" in His own language, Aramaic, it did not sound harsh or brusk as it does in our current English. Instead, it was a title of respect, which He also used when He hung on the cross and committed Mary to John's keeping (John 19:26, 27).

3 How did Jesus live up to His mother's expectations? Back in 1:3 we learned that all things were made through Jesus. What was God trying to tell everyone when Jesus displayed His unusual capability and authority over those waterpots?

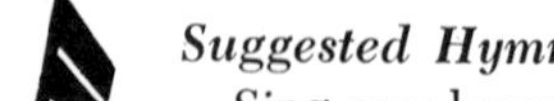

Suggested Hymn

Sing any hymn you know that reflects the Christian's joy, such as "Jesus Loves Even Me," p. 492, *Great Hymns of the Faith*.

Prayer

JOHN 2:13–25

5

Prayer

Thank You, Father, that the Bible is not just men's thoughts, but that all Scripture is given inspiration of God.

Read Scripture

Each year the Jewish people celebrated an important religious feast, the Passover—as they still do.

Questions

1 Where did Jesus go when He arrived in Jerusalem?
2 What did He see there?
3 How did this make Him feel? Why? (Remember the temple was planned by God—the place where His presence dwelt among men. It was a very holy place.) What did Jesus do?
4 Who challenged His right to do this?
5 What answer did He give them?
6 Did they understand what He meant? (Really He was saying, "The sign of who I am and of My authority will be the cross and My Resurrection.")
7 Apparently Jesus performed miracles while He was in Jerusalem. What effect did this have on the people who saw them?
8 As verse 25 tells us, Jesus could see whether these people believed He was just a miracle worker or really the Son of God. What do you believe about Jesus? What difference does it make what a person believes?

Prayer

"Do you not know that you are God's temple and that God's Spirit dwells in you?" (1 Corinthians 3:16). Dear Lord, please help us to remember this truth. *Amen.*

JESUS AND NICODEMUS—JOHN 3:1–21

6

Opening Prayer

1 Short prayer by head of household or person he chooses.
2 Thank God for the opportunity to gather together as a family for Bible study.
3 Ask God for help in understanding the passage.

Introduction

The Pharisees were a Jewish religious party that practiced strict obedience to the Law of Moses and other traditional regulations. They believed God's grace was achieved this way. Jesus denounced them for their self-righteousness, hypocrisy, and concern for minute details of the Law while disregarding important points.

First Scripture Reading

John 3:1–13

Leader selects one family member to read what Nicodemus says and another to read what Jesus says. Read with expression.

Questions

1 Who came one night to visit Jesus?
2 In verse 4, what question did Nicodemus ask?
3 How can you enter the Kingdom of God?
4 What does that mean to you?

Second Scripture Reading

John 3:14–21

Point out key verse, John 3:16, 17.

Questions

1 How can we have eternal life?
2 Why do men love the darkness?
3 God sent Jesus into the world to be our ______.

Prayer (Mother)

Thank God for telling us how to enter His Kingdom and for giving us eternal life through Jesus Christ.

JOHN 3:22–36

7

Prayer

Scripture Reading

John 3:22–36

Questions

1 If John the Baptist testified that he was not the Messiah, then who was he?
2 What does verse 24 tell us awaits John? (*See* Mark 6:17–29.)
3 Whose baptisms drew the bigger crowds? How did John react to this?
4 What happens to those who believe on the Son? What about those that believeth not the Son?

Prayer

Lord, help us to find real happiness in pointing people to You as John did. *Amen.*

SAMARITAN WOMAN AT THE WELL—JOHN 4:1–26

8

Prayer

Introduction

It was time for Jesus to head north from Judea, going toward Galilee. Most Jewish travelers would have stayed on the eastern bank of the Jordan River, going through the province of Perea, rather than heading due north through Samaria. Check this on a Bible map.

Read Scripture

Questions

1 How did the Jews and the Samaritans feel about each other (4:9)? The Samaritans were a mixed race of Jews and Gentiles. Their religion was based on the five Books of Moses (Pentateuch) alone. Through the years great bitterness and hatred had grown up between these neighbors.

2 What do you learn of Jesus' attitude toward people outside the Jewish circle? Are there people of a different background and/or race that you have little or no use for? How would Jesus want you to feel about them?

3 Most women came to the well to draw water for their families in the early morning and the evening. This woman came at noon, when no one was ordinarily around. How did Jesus start a conversation? What was the woman's great need (v. 14)? How did Jesus help her?

4 What wonderful thing did Jesus reveal about Himself (4:26)?

5 Notice the effect her testimony had on others (4:41, 42).

Suggested Hymn

"I Heard the Voice of Jesus Say," p. 225, *Great Hymns of the Faith;* p. 199, *Inspiring Hymns.*

Prayer

JESUS HEALS THE NOBLEMAN'S SON—JOHN 4:46–54

9

Opening Prayer

Scripture Reading

Questions

1 What town is Jesus presently in? What miracle had already taken place here?

2 What did the nobleman ask of Jesus? What town was his son in?

3 What do you feel Jesus meant in verse 48 "Except ye see signs and wonders, ye will not believe"? Notice that our

Lord addressed him in the plural number. He did not say, "Except *thou* see signs."

4 Did Jesus do exactly what the man asked of Him? Did He give him a sign? What did He tell the man? (*See* Matthew 12:39; 16:4.)

5 Are we told that the man believed Jesus and went on his way? (The distance between Cana and Capernaum is at least twenty to thirty miles.) Why do you feel the man believed what Jesus told him?

6 At what exact time was the boy healed? Why is this so important?

7 What became of the family after the miracles in verse 53?

8 What are the dangers of trusting in miracles only?

Closing Prayer

Lord, help us to trust You even when we don't see great things happening. Help us to learn to obey You as well as to believe in You. *Amen.*

JESUS HEALS THE SICK MAN AT THE POOL—JOHN 5:1–18

10

Opening Prayer

1 Leader prays for the Holy Spirit to guide the family Bible study and to teach the messages God wants each one to learn.

2 Prayer requests may be asked for here.

Introduction

What is a miracle? Look it up in a good dictionary. (It is a wonder, sign, event attesting to the power of God.)

Scripture Reading

John 5:1–18

The Sabbath is the seventh day of the week in the Jewish calendar, the period from Friday evening to Saturday evening, a day of rest and worship.

Questions

1 Where did this take place?

2 Why was there a large crowd of sick people lying on the porches?

3 What were they waiting for?

4 Who in particular did Jesus notice?

5 How long had he been sick?
6 What did Jesus command him to do?
7 Then what happened to the sick man?
8 Why did the Jews begin to persecute Jesus and determine to kill him?

(For further discussion ask family members to tell about other miracles Jesus performed.)

Closing Prayer

1 Leader chooses someone to pray.
2 Thank God for this recorded miracle showing Jesus' power over sickness and time.
3 Pray for someone who is sick and/or thank God for someone who has been healed.

JOHN 5:19–40

11

Prayer

Father, please make Your Word alive to us today. *Amen.*

Introduction

Jesus was talking to some religious leaders. They were angry with Him and were sure that He was only a fake. They would not believe that He was who He claimed to be: God's Son.

Scripture Reading

Questions

1 Make a list of the things Jesus told these men about the relationship between Him and His Father, God. (There are about eight. How many can you find in verses 19–30?)
2 If He were only a man, could He make these claims?
3 A *witness* is a person who tells that he knows something is true, or untrue. In verses 31–40 (LB), Jesus said there were three witnesses to prove His claims about Himself. Can you name them? (Each one of these said the same thing: that Jesus came from God.)
4 Wherever Jesus went there were two opposite reactions to Him. What were they? Do you think people are like this today when they hear the Gospel?
5 What did Jesus say is the final destiny of those who believe in Him. Of those who do not? Can you think of someone who is not yet a Christian for whom you could begin to pray?

Prayer

Dear Lord, we thank You that You sent Jesus to our world to make eternal life possible for anyone who will believe in Him. *Amen.*

JESUS FEEDS 5,000 PEOPLE—JOHN 6:1–14, 25–35

12

Opening Prayer

1 Leader asks God for wisdom and guidance while studying this passage.
2 Ask that God's messages be understood by the family and applied by the Holy Spirit in their lives.
3 Prayer Requests

Introduction

The Gospels of Matthew, Mark, and Luke also record this event. However, John goes further and teaches us the spiritual meaning. This study is in two parts.

(Picture the scene—Jesus and His disciples crossing the lake, climbing a hill, and sitting down on the grass, all the time being followed by a large crowd.)

Read Scripture

John 6:1–14. Leader asks the oldest child to read.

Questions

1 Why was the crowd following Jesus?
2 What did Jesus ask Philip?
3 How much food did they have?
4 What did Jesus do with the bread and fish?
5 Was there enough food for everyone?

Introduction

After Jesus fed the 5,000, He went to Capernaum the next day. The crowds looked for Him and found Him.

Scripture Reading (John 6:25–35)

Questions

1 Why are the people looking for Jesus?
2 What kind of food does He tell them to work for?
3 What kind of work does God want us to do?
4 What kind of bread does God give?
5 What kind of bread did Moses give his people in the desert?
6 Who is "the bread of life"?

MEMORY VERSE John 6:35

1 All read Jesus' words in verse 35 together.

2 Or Father or Mother reads, "I am the bread of life [Jesus told them]; he who comes to me shall not hunger, and he who believes in me shall never thirst" (RSV).
3 Leader asks child who can write to copy the memory verse on an index card. Family decides where to display the card.

Closing Prayer

1 Leader asks someone to pray.
2 Thank God for the food He provides for our bodies and the food He provides for our souls, for Jesus Christ, who is the Bread of Life. *Amen.*

THE LORD WALKS ON THE SEA—JOHN 6:15–21

13

Opening Prayer

Scripture Reading

Questions

1 What plans did the people have for Jesus in verse 15? Why did they feel they had to use force?
2 Where did Jesus go? What do you think He wanted to do?
3 Where did the disciples go at nightfall? Why do you think Jesus had left His friends on their own?
4 What happened to make the disciples so terrified while rowing the boat? Why were they so frightened at seeing Jesus? Did they think He would drown?
5 What words did Jesus call to them?
6 What things make you feel frightened? How do you calm your fears?
7 Should a Christian be frightened by a lot of things?

Closing Prayer

Remind us always, Lord, that You are in control all the time. We, like the disciples, so quickly forget that You are in command of all things. Help us to depend on You not only during good times but when things are difficult and dangerous. *Amen.*

JOHN 6:22–40

14

Prayer

Summary

The previous day Jesus had performed a miracle by feeding a crowd of people with just a boy's lunch. The people then said that Jesus was the Promised Prophet, their Messiah, and they wanted to make Him their king. He had left them to be alone for a while. Then, walking on the water, He had joined His disciples who were crossing the lake in a ship.

Read Scripture

Questions

CHILDREN Who were all the people looking for? Where did they find Him?

TEEN-AGERS What did Jesus say was the real reason the people were looking for Him? What kind of food should they really be seeking?

ADULTS Who is the Bread of Life? How does Jesus explain this eternal food in contrast to the bread the people had eaten the day before and in the desert with Moses? What must people do to receive everlasting life?

MEMORY VERSE Verse 37: "All that the Father giveth me shall come to me; and him that cometh to me I will in no wise cast out."

Sing

Choose a song which tells about the Bread of Life . . . how Jesus receives all who come to Him and satisfies the hunger of the soul.

Prayer

Pray especially for people you may know who may be hungry for the Bread of Life. Each member of the family may want to lead in prayer remembering a special friend.

JOHN 6:41–51

15

Prayer

Read Scripture

Summary

John had just completed the miracle of the loaves and fishes for the hungry five thousand people. He then tells them of a bread that comes down from heaven (v. 41) and if they eat it they will never be hungry again.

Questions

1 Turn in your Bibles to John 6 and read verses 41–44.
 a Who did Jesus say He was?

b Why didn't the Jews believe that Jesus came down from heaven?
c How did Jesus answer the questioning Jews?
d What will Christ do for those who come to Him (v. 44)?

2 Now read verses 45 and 46.
a Every person who knows God also comes to whom?
b Who is the only one who has ever seen God?

3 Read verses 47–51.
a What do we receive when we believe in Jesus?
b What does Jesus call Himself?
c What does He mean by saying that He is the Bread of Life (vs. 49–50)?

Personal Sharing Time

In order to grow strong and healthy, we must first know that we feel hungry; then we must eat the food that we receive (no one else can eat it for us). The food then becomes a part of us giving us energy and strength. How can we compare eating food to having Jesus become a part of our life?

Prayer

Thank the Lord for the food that we eat, but more than that thank Him for Jesus, the Bread of Life, who gives us strength and power to live each day for Him.

JOHN 7:37–52

16

Prayer

Read Scripture

John 7:37–52

Questions

CHILDREN Did the people agree about who Jesus was? Who did they think He was?

TEEN-AGERS From what town was the Christ to come, according to Old Testament Scriptures? What did the Pharisees want to do to Jesus?

ADULTS What promise did Jesus give? What is the living water He provides? Who were to receive the Holy Spirit?

CROSS-REFERENCES See Leviticus 23:33–36, 42, 43 for the observance of the Feast of Tabernacles. (*See* John 3 for more information about Nicodemus.)

Discuss

Try to put yourself in the place of the Jews who heard Jesus on the last day of the feast. What do you think your reaction would have been?

Prayer

(Reference: *Christ in All the Scriptures* by A. M. Hodgkin.)

THE WOMAN TAKEN IN ADULTERY JESUS, THE LIGHT OF THE WORLD— JOHN 8:1–30

17

Prayer

Introduction

Verse 1–11 Although there is strong internal and external evidence that this incident was not included in John's original account, it is unquestionable that it forms part of the authentic teaching of the Church, and may have been inserted to illustrate Jesus' statement in 8:15, "I judge no man."

This incident takes place shortly before the event of His Crucifixion.

Read Scripture

John 8:1–30

Questions

What is the setting? Who are the accusers? Is their accusation aimed at the woman or at Jesus? How does He handle the Pharisees, the accused woman? Why do you think all the men slipped away? How did the woman leave?

Introduction

Verses 12–30 The relationship between Jesus and the religious leaders was getting worse. Jesus had just escaped arrest (7:32), had outfoxed them in a test (8:3–11), and had answered their objection to His testimony (8:13). They next resorted to personal insult by asking three questions aimed at resisting the truth rather than finding it. Try to understand what His enemies were driving at, and how Jesus answered them.

Questions

1 "Where is your father?" (8:19 RSV). Hadn't Jesus explained about a second witness to His claims? It may even have been a slur on His earthly family, stirring up gossip that

Joseph was not really His father. (Jesus' answer is in verse 19.)

2 "Will he kill himself?" (8:22). Jews believed that all who committed suicide went to the lowest part of Hades. They were wishing He would "go to hell." (Jesus' answer is in verses 21, 23.)

3 "Who are you?" (8:25). Think of all the truth about Himself Jesus had just shared with them. Having ears, they heard not (Mark 8:18). Such a question showed they had rejected it all. (Jesus' answer is in verses 25, 26.)

4 Summarize the things Jesus told about Himself. What was His chief purpose (8:29)?

In His effort to describe Himself to human beings, God had used the expression "I am" (Exodus 3:14), denoting the eternal present existence. While speaking to the people at the Temple, Jesus continued to do this. Notice 8:12, 23, 24, 28.

Further Study (optional)

Try collecting information on the seven "I Am" sayings found in the Gospel of John.

John	6:35	Bread of Life
	8:12, 9:5	Light of the World
	10:7, 9	Door
	10:11, 14	Good Shepherd
	11:25	Resurrection and the Life
	14:6	Way, Truth, and Life
	15:1, 5	True Vine

Suggested Hymn

"The Light of the World Is Jesus," p. 213, *Great Hymns of the Faith;* p. 335, *Inspiring Hymns.*

Prayer

(Reference: *Portraits of Christ* by Henry Gariepy.)

THREE-FATHERS DISCUSSION—JOHN 8:31–59

18

Prayer

Read Scripture

Questions

1 Three fathers are listed in this section. Tell what things you learn about Father Abraham, God the Father, and "their" father the Devil.

2 What purposes lay behind this discussion between Jesus and the religious leaders (8:40, 49)?
3 What did Jesus teach about being free, about truth, death, and sin?
4 He used the personal pronoun "I" many times. What claims did He make for Himself?

The climax of Jesus' claims infuriated the Pharisees so much that they picked up stones with which to pelt Him to death. It was that grand and sweeping statement in v. 58, "Before Abraham was, I am." This had a familiar ring, because this was the name God had called Himself when Moses inquired in Exodus 3:14. Jesus was present and accounted for *before* their honored ancestor ever appeared on the human scene.

Suggested Hymn

"Hallelujah, What a Savior," p. 127, *Great Hymns of the Faith;* p. 302, *Inspiring Hymns.*

Prayer

Give thanks that Jesus came to show us the Father.

JESUS HEALS THE MAN BORN BLIND—JOHN 9:1–41

19

Opening Prayer

Scripture Reading

This is the only case on record of our Lord dealing with a congenital disease. There may have been others, but this is the only one recorded.

Questions

1 What did the disciples think caused the blindness in the beggar? How did Jesus answer them?
2 How are we told the blind man made his living?
3 How did Jesus heal the man? Since Jesus could have healed him immediately, why do you think He told him to go to the pool?
4 On what day of the week did the healing take place?
5 Where was the blind man taken after being healed? What was asked of him? What did he reply? Who did the blind man think Jesus was?
6 Why did the Jews feel Jesus was not from God in verse 16? What sort of things do you do on the Sabbath?

7 What was asked of the beggar's parents? How did they reply? Why were they afraid of the Jews in verse 22?
8 After the blind man had been summoned for the second time to tell his story—how did he provoke the Jews in verse 27?
9 When Jesus found out that the man had been cast out of the synagogue, He found him and asked him what question? How did the blind man react?

Discussion

What do you think Jesus means in verses 39, 40, 41?

Closing Prayer

Saviour, we praise You because You are alive and our souls are safe with You when our human bodies have to die. *Amen.*

THE PARABLE OF THE SHEEPFOLD—JOHN 10:1–18

20

Opening Prayer

Introduction

Since Palestine was familiar with raising and caring of sheep, it was natural for Jesus to compare the care which a shepherd gives his sheep to the way he cared for His disciples. Jesus says in John 21:16, "Tend my sheep" (RSV). Interestingly, our word for *Pastor* comes from the Latin word for *shepherd.*

Sheep were kept at night in a sheepfold so no harm could befall them. The fold was surrounded by a wall and was entered only by a guarded door. The gatekeeper admitted only those shepherds whose flocks were kept in that fold.

Scripture Reading

Questions

1 Who does not enter the sheepfold by the door?
2 Who does enter in by the door?
3 Do sheep recognize their own shepherd?
4 Would they ever follow a stranger?
5 Who is the door of the sheepfold? What happens to those who pass through this door?
6 What does the Good Shepherd do in verse 11?
7 Who abandons the sheep in verses 12, 13?
8 In verses 14, 15, what does Jesus say about His Father and His sheep?

9 Who are the "other sheep" referred to in verse 16?

10 What superhuman claim does Jesus make in verse 18?

11 Jesus knows us by name. How can we learn to recognize His voice? How do you think Jesus would recognize a Christian?

Closing Prayer

Lord, we thank You for knowing each of us so well. We are so powerless against the evil one, and over our sinful natures. Please give us Your protection and help to fight these problems. In Your Name, we ask this. *Amen.*

JOHN 10:25–30

21

Prayer

Begin with a prayer that the Holy Spirit open up the Scripture and discussion.

Scripture Reading

To be read from the Living Bible or Living New Testament (if at all possible).

In John 10:11–15, Jesus describes Himself as the "Good Shepherd."

Questions

1 According to verse 27, what three things do we learn about Jesus' true sheep?

2 What does it mean to you to follow Jesus? In school—at work—at home—in the neighborhood—on the job? Discuss.

3 Everyone wants to feel safe and secure. The dictionary describes *secure* as: Free from fear, care, or anxiety. What beautiful picture of Jesus, the Father, and His sheep (those who belong to Him) do we see in verses 28, 29? Take a minute to picture this in your mind and then have someone put it in his own words. (Several members of the family might even like to dramatize this "picture.")

4 Who might want to "snatch" us away from Jesus? Have you ever been tempted NOT to follow Jesus? Discuss. Philippians 1:6 says: ". . . he who began a good work in you will bring it to completion at the day of Jesus Christ" (RSV).

5 If Jesus will keep us safe and secure in Himself, what is our part?

6 From verse 30, what do we learn about Jesus' relationship with His Father?

Prayer

Remembering Jesus' power to keep us safe from the evil one, pray that the Holy Spirit will help us to *want* to continue to trust in, to cling to, and to rely on Jesus.

LAZARUS RAISED FROM THE DEAD—JOHN 11:1–44

22

Opening Prayer

Scripture Reading

Questions

1 Who sent the message to Jesus and what was it about? What did Jesus reply?

2 What does Jesus tell us about the illness in verse 4?

Jesus had a special affection for Lazarus which is repeated in verses 3, 5, 11, 36. He is the only man named in the entire Gospel of John for whom Jesus is said to have had a personal love.

3 Why then, did he tarry for two days before leaving for Bethany?

4 What was the misunderstanding between the apostles and Jesus?

5 What do you think Thomas meant in verse 16 when he said, "Let us also go, that we may die with him"?

6 What do verses 25, 26 mean personally to you? Do you think most of your friends know about this?

7 Do you think that Martha had decided it was too late for Jesus to save Lazarus?

8 Was Jesus unhappy when He got to the grave? What are we told He did? Why do you think He asked where Lazarus was buried?

9 How long had Lazarus been in the tomb when Jesus arrived?

10 What must one do in order to see the glory of God (verse 40)?

11 In the end, what happens to Lazarus? What does this miracle show us?

Closing Prayer

Lord, we thank You that You came into our world to show us that You have power over death. We give You thanks for Your wonderful gift of a new and never-ending life with You as our Saviour and Friend. *Amen.*

THE FAREWELL SUPPER AT BETHANY— JOHN 11:55–57; 12:1–18

23

Opening Prayer

Scripture Reading

Questions

1 In verse 55, what did the people have to do in order to observe the feast?

2 What did the "Sanhedrin" (The Chief Priests and Pharisees) want to do with Jesus?

In the wilderness, Jesus was quietly spending the period with His disciples while the city was filling up with crowds coming for the feast.

3 Where did Jesus go six days before the Passover?

4 Who was Lazarus? What was Martha doing at the gathering?

5 Who was the center of interest in 12:3? What did Mary do? Why did she do what she did?

6 With what type of perfume did Mary anoint Jesus?

This oil was very costly. Verse 5 means that its worth equaled an unskilled laborer's wages for three hundred days.

7 Who objected to Mary's act? Did his objection sound reasonable? What type of person was Judas? What do you think was really behind his protest?

8 What did Jesus reply to Judas? What do you think Jesus means regarding the poor people (v. 8)?

Closing Prayer

Lord, help us today and everyday to remember what are the important things in our lives and to always remember to put You first and then, as You promise us, all other good things will be added. *Amen.*

THE TRIUMPHAL ENTRY—JOHN 12:12–19

24

Prayer

Introduction

As Jesus approaches Jerusalem, the crowds begin to claim Him as their Messiah and King who came to free them from the Romans.

Read Scripture

Questions

1 Turn to John 12 and read verses 12, 13.
  a How did the people welcome Jesus as He was on His way to Jerusalem?
  b What did they cry out to Him?
2 Now read verses 14–16.
  a On what animal did Jesus ride?
  b What did the disciples come to realize about this after Jesus had gone to heaven?
3 Read verses 17–19.
  a What was the main reason for so many people going out to meet Jesus in this way?
  b How did the Pharisees feel about Jesus being so popular?

Personal Sharing Time

These people were praising Jesus even though they didn't know very much about Him and had not benefited from His marvelous plan of salvation as we have. Discuss some ways that you as a family and as individuals can praise the Lord and bring honor to His Name. Name some of the many things for which you can praise Him.

Prayer

Thank Jesus that He is our Saviour, and ask Him to help you to be always praising Him for the miracles that He performs each day for us.

JOHN 12:23–33

25

Prayer

Introduction

After the triumphal entry, Jesus tells the people that He must die in order to fulfill God's purpose.

Read Scripture

Questions

1 Turn in your Bibles to John 12 and read verses 23–26.
  a What does Jesus say is going to happen to Him (v. 23)?
  b How does Jesus compare Himself with a kernel of wheat?
  c How does Jesus say we should feel about our life on this earth?

   d What must a servant of Jesus do?
2 Now read verses 27, 28.
   a How does Jesus feel as the time approaches for Him to die (27)?
   b What does Jesus ask the Father?
   c What is God's answer?
3 Read verses 29–33.
   a From whom did the people think God's voice came?
   b For what reason did God speak?
   c Who did Jesus say would be cast out?
   d What would Jesus' death accomplish (v. 32)?

Personal Sharing Time

In verse 25, Jesus asks us to be willing to give up our lives for His sake. Although He seldom asks this of us, He does ask that we be willing to give up other things in our lives that would keep us from being able to fully follow Him. Can you think of anything in your life that might stand in the way of your being close to Jesus? (For example, friends that don't love Him, TV programs, bad habits, wasted time, money.)

Prayer

Thank Jesus for giving His life for you and ask Him to make you willing to give your all for Him.

JOHN 12:34–43

26

Prayer

Introduction

The people who had followed Jesus from Jerusalem were both astonished and disappointed that Jesus was going to die. They had thought of Him as their earthly King. They failed to understand that through His death they would receive eternal life, and they turned against Him.

Scripture Reading

Questions

1 Turn in your Bibles to John 12 and read verses 34–36.
   a Explain the confusion (v. 34) of the people who had followed Jesus.
   b How did Jesus answer their questions (v. 35, 36)? Who is the light He is talking about?
2 Now read verses 37–41.
   a How did the people feel about Jesus?

   b Who prophesied many years ago that this would happen?
3 Read verses 42, 43.
   a Why didn't those who did believe in Jesus tell anyone so?
   b Whose praise did these people choose?
   c How can this apply to you?

Personal Sharing Time

The people who followed and praised Jesus as He rode home on the donkey from Jerusalem thought He was going to be their earthly King. When He explained to them that He was going to die before becoming their heavenly King, they no longer wanted Him. They were only interested in satisfying their immediate needs. Sometimes we, too, are interested in only our immediate desires and forget to think about eternal values. Can you think of some ways that this is true in your life?

Prayer

Thank Jesus for our eternal life and ask Him to help us to realize that our first goal should be to serve Him.

JOHN 12:44–50

27

Prayer

Scripture Reading

Questions

1 Did Jesus come to judge the world?
2 In seeing Jesus, who does one see also?
3 Did the claims of Jesus originate with Him? If not, from whom did they come?
4 Why is it so serious a matter to reject Jesus?
5 What did Jesus mean by saying He was the Light?

Prayer

JOHN 13:1–20

28

Prayer

Father, help us not to be dull of mind and heart as we read Your Word today.

Introduction

This is the last Passover meal Jesus takes with His men. The next day is the day of His Crucifixion.

Read Scripture

Questions

1. Four times in this section are the words, "Jesus knew" or "Jesus knowing." What does it say He knew?
2. Does He act or talk like a man who knows He will be killed within twenty-four hours?
3. Is there any indication Jesus is thinking of Himself? Of whom is He thinking?

4. What does He do? Why does He do this? (It was customary for a servant in a house to wash the feet of guests when they came in. Apparently, there had been no servant in this place to do it.)
5. Do you think it says anything about the twelve disciples that none of them offered to take the towel from Jesus and do the footwashing?
6. As a family, how can we follow Christ's example of serving one another instead of expecting to be served? Let each member suggest one specific way.

Prayer

Dear Lord, please help us to remember Your great lesson in humility, and to be willing to serve others for Your sake. *Amen.*

JOHN 13:21–38

29

Prayer

Father, please open our eyes to the wonder of Your Word. *Amen.*

Read Scripture

Questions

1. We read that now Jesus felt a great "anguish" (troubling) of spirit. Do you think this was because of fear of the cross, or because the person who was going to betray Him was one of His own men—or some other reason?
2. How do you think the disciples felt when Jesus said, "One of you will betray me"?
3. Is there any indication that any of them suspected who the traitor might be? (Even after Jesus gave him the morsel and told him to hurry?)

4 Before this night, Judas had already arranged to betray Christ (*see* Matthew 26:14–16). How do you think Judas felt as he left the lighted room and his companions and went out into the dark?
5 As Jesus thought of what was just ahead of Him, did He think of it all as a disaster? How did He describe it?
6 What did He say He wanted His men to do, after He was gone? How much?
7 The mark of a Christian then, as now, is not church membership or a bumper sticker but is love. Take a couple of minutes and memorize verse 35, and pray that God will help your family to be more loving.

Prayer

JESUS IS THE WAY, THE TRUTH, THE LIFE—JOHN 14:1–9

30

Opening Prayer

1 A short prayer by head of household or someone he asks to pray.
2 Ask God for wisdom and guidance in understanding this passage from John.
3 Pray for the application in lives of each family member by God's Holy Spirit.

Introduction

It was the day before the Feast of the Passover and Jesus and the disciples were at supper. Judas left. Jesus explained to the disciples that He would leave them soon and they could not follow right away, but later. Peter asked, "Lord, where are you going?" (John 13:36 RSV). They could not understand.

Scripture Reading

John 14:1–9

Questions

1 What did Jesus tell His disciples not to be?
2 What should they do?
3 What did He say about His Father's house?
4 Will Jesus be all alone in heaven?
5 Who will be with Him?
6 How did Jesus say we get to heaven?
7 If we know Jesus, who do we know?
8 Comments and further discussion.

MEMORY VERSE John 14:6 (RSV). "Jesus said to him: 'I am the way, and the truth, and the life; no one comes to the Father, but by me.'"

Leader asks for a volunteer or selects a family member to write verse on a card for display for memorizing.

Closing Prayer

1 Short prayer by different members of family.
2 Thank God for the opportunity to study His Word and for preparing a place in heaven for us through Jesus Christ.

JOHN 14:15–31

31

Prayer

Begin with a prayer that the Holy Spirit open up your hearts to the Scripture and discussion.

Scripture Reading

To be read from the Living Bible or Living New Testament (if at all possible).

Questions

1 Jesus talks about our love for Him in verses 15, 21. If we really love Him, what does the Scripture say we will do? What will Jesus do? What about the Father?
2 Throughout the Bible, we read how important it is to God that we don't just TALK about loving Him, but that we SHOW our love for Him by our obedience. (*See also* Luke 6:46.) Sometimes it isn't easy to obey God. The disciples had Jesus physically close to them to help them obey, but who did Jesus send to take His place on earth to help us? (*See* verses 16, 17.)
3 From verses 16, 17, 26, what do we learn about the Holy Spirit (the Comforter)?
4 Many times we get filled with fear, or when things seem to go wrong, we are tempted to be troubled or afraid. Verse 27 tells that Jesus left us a gift to keep us from feeling that way. What is that gift? In order to make any gift our own, what do we have to do?

   Verse 27 in the Amplified Bible says: "Peace I leave with you . . . stop allowing yourselves to be agitated and disturbed; and do not permit yourselves to be fearful and intimidated and cowardly and unsettled."

5 How do we know from verses 30, 31 that Satan didn't have Jesus killed, but that Jesus *gave up* His own life?

Prayer Suggestion

Remembering God's great love and power—and His gift of peace—pray that the Holy Spirit will help us to love and obey God and that the Holy Spirit will make His peace real in our hearts so we are no longer afraid or troubled.

JESUS IS THE VINE AND WE ARE THE BRANCHES—JOHN 15:1–17

32

Opening Prayer (Father)

Almighty God, help us find out what John 15:1–17 says. Give us wisdom to understand it, and apply the truths we learn in our lives, in the Name of Jesus Christ. *Amen.*

Introduction (Father)

In this passage, Jesus uses the illustration of a vine and a gardener. To prune a plant is to cut off the useless branches.

Scripture Reading (Teen-ager)

John 15:1–17. Others follow silently in their Bibles.

Questions (Mother)

FOR CHILD

1 Who is the vine and who is the gardener?

2 What does the gardener do to the plant?

FOR TEEN-AGER

1 How can a Christian bear fruit? (In Galatians 5:22, 23, we find that ". . . the fruit of the Spirit is love, joy, peace, longsuffering, kindness, goodness, faithfulness, meekness, self-control . . ." ASV.)

2 Who are the branches?

3 What happens if we remain in Christ?

FOR ADULT

1 How is God's glory shown?

2 How can we stay in Jesus' love?

3 What command does Jesus give in verses 12, 17?

4 What does Jesus call those people who do what He commands?

MEMORY VERSE John 15:5

Closing Prayer (Child)

Our Father in Heaven, thank You for Your written Word, the Bible. Help us to abide in Jesus, to bear good fruit, and to love one another, in Jesus' Name. *Amen.*

LOVE—JOHN 15:8–17

33

Prayer

Summary

Shortly before Jesus was crucified He had long, intimate talks with His disciples. Here John has recorded some of Jesus' final words to them about love.

Scripture Reading

John 15:8–17

Questions

TRUE OR FALSE

1 Jesus kept His Father's Commandments.
2 Joy does not result in keeping God's Commandments.
3 Jesus said His Commandment is that we love one another.
4 Giving one's life for another is not a sign of love.
5 Jesus did not call His disciples friends.
6 Jesus chose His disciples and wanted them to have fruitful lives.

Discuss

How do obedience and love work together? How do we show our love to one another in our family?

Prayer

(Reference: For more reading about love, *The Miracle of Love* by Charles L. Allen; *And the Greatest of These* by George Sweeting.)

THE WORK OF THE HOLY SPIRIT—JOHN 16:1–16

34

Opening Prayer

Introduction

There should really be no break between chapters 15 and 16. The theme of the world's hostility to Jesus and the disciples continues in this chapter.

Scripture Reading

Questions

1 Why did Jesus warn His disciples in advance why they must suffer in verse 1?
2 What are the disciples to do when hardship comes (verse 4a)?
3 Why did Jesus not have to warn them of future hardships while He was with them (verse 4b)?
4 How did the disciples feel at the prospect of Jesus' departure?
5 Why will it be to their advantage for Jesus to depart?
6 In what three ways would the Holy Spirit convince the unbelieving world that its attitude toward Jesus has been wrong (verses 9–11)?
7 Who is the "prince of this world" (v. 11)? What does he do to you?
8 In verse 12, Jesus says "I have yet many things to say unto you, but ye cannot bear them now." A wonderful principle is revealed here—Jesus reveals things to us only as we can bear the revelation. Can you think of any examples in your own life?

Closing Prayer

We thank You God as we look back at our own lives that You did not tell us all about it at the beginning, but that You teach us as much as we are able to bear. *Amen.*

JOHN 16:16–33

35

Prayer

Begin with a prayer that the Holy Spirit open up your hearts to the Scripture and discussion.

Scripture Reading

To be read from the Living Bible or Living New Testament (if at all possible).

Questions

1 What do you think Jesus meant when He said, "In just a little while I will be gone, and you will see me no more; but just a little while after that, and you will see me again!" (16:16 LB). Discuss. (*See also* John 13:1–3; 10:17.)

2 What do we learn about prayer from verse 23? Why is it so important to use Jesus' name when we pray? 1 Timothy 2:5 (RSV) says, "For there is one God, and there is one mediator between God and men, the man Christ Jesus . . . ."
3 In John 16:17, the disciples were full of questions just as we are until we really "see" Jesus as who He is. But Jesus wants us to see and know Him as He really is. What promise do we have in verse 24?
4 There are times when those we love cannot be with us and we're left all alone. Verse 32 tells us that this happened to Jesus, also, but what wonderful thing do we learn from this verse?
5 Many people think that if someone belongs to Jesus, he will never again have any trials or sorrows. This isn't what verse 33 says, but what wonderful promise do we have instead? Have you ever allowed Jesus to bring you through a trial or problem? Discuss. (*See also* John 14:27.)

Prayer Suggestion

Remembering that God wants us to come to Him in Jesus' Name, and that He wants us to know Him as He really is, and that He will never leave us or forsake us—pray that we might ask to know Him better and that we might know His peace in the midst of loneliness or trouble.

JESUS PRAYS FOR HIS FOLLOWERS—JOHN 17:1–10

36

Opening Prayer (Mother)

Our Father in Heaven, help us to understand these verses. Give us wisdom and an open mind while we read, and listen, and discuss, so that we can learn more about You, in Jesus' Name we pray. *Amen.*

Introduction (Mother)

Jesus knew that soon He would be crucified. Judas had left to betray Him. The eleven disciples listened to Jesus speak this great showing of love which He had for them, and for us, in this prayer to His Father, God.

Scripture Reading

John 17:1–26

Leader reads the whole prayer and others follow in their Bibles.

Questions (Leader)

Questions in this study are on verses 1–10.

FOR CHILD 1 Who sent Jesus into the world to give us eternal life?

2 Who is praying this prayer?

FOR TEEN-AGER 1 Why does Jesus ask for God's glory?

2 What does Jesus say about the work God gave Him to do on earth?

FOR ADULT 1 To whom did Jesus give God's message?

2 What did they do with it?

FOR EVERYONE Who is Jesus praying for? Why?

Closing Prayer (Leader)

Dear God, thank You for this beautiful prayer and all that Jesus has done for us for Your glory, in His Name, we thank You. *Amen.*

JOHN 17:1–12

36A

Prayer

Begin with a prayer that the Holy Spirit open up the Scripture and discussion.

Scripture Reading

Jesus' prayer to His Father before His Crucifixion. To be read in the Living Bible or Living New Testament.

Questions

1 In verses 1, 4 and 5, Jesus talks about glory. The dictionary describes glory as: exalted praise and honor. According to verse 1, why did Jesus ask His Father to reveal His glory? (Notice how Jesus never kept the glory for Himself.) What wonderful truth do we learn about Jesus in verse 5?

2 From verse 2, what do we learn about the power and authority that God has given to Jesus?

3 Read verse 3 in various other Bible translations. (Living Bible is a paraphrase and is not particularly clear on verse 3.)

What do the words "eternal life" mean to each of you? Discuss. Note that most translations of the Bible describe *eternal life* as "knowing" God and Jesus Christ whom He has sent. Does this differ from what you previously thought about eternal life? What does it mean to "know" God? Discuss. Notice that the Scripture does *not* say to "know about"

God. What's the difference between *knowing* someone and *knowing about* someone?

4 According to verse 7, from where did everything that Jesus possessed come?

5 If Jesus, who was the Son of God, still had to rely completely on His Father for everything, what about us; on whom should we be depending?

6 Do you depend on God all the time or only for the "big" things, or when you're in trouble? Discuss.

Prayer Suggestion

Remembering that Jesus who was God's only Son spent much time in prayer and that God wants us to really "know" Him and depend on Him—pray that He will help us to spend more time with Him in prayer and that we will remember to depend on Him for everything.

JOHN 17:13–26

37

Prayer

Begin with a prayer that the Holy Spirit open up the Scripture and discussion.

Scripture Reading

To be read in the Living Bible or Living New Testament. A continuation of Jesus' prayer to His Father before Crucifixion.

Questions

1 What was Jesus' specific prayer for His disciples, for *us* and for all who have accepted Him as their Saviour, in verses 15, 21?

2 How can we be sure that He wasn't just praying for His disciples of that day, but that He was praying for us also? (*See* verse 20.)

3 What do you think Jesus means in verses 15, 16 by saying that if we are really His followers, we are no longer part of this world? In what way are we no longer part of the world; we still live here, don't we? Discuss. (*See* Romans 12:2.)

4 Many times we don't realize the importance of studying the Bible. According to Jesus in verse 17 (LB), what happens to us as we *prayerfully* study God's Word? What promise does He give us in verse 19?

5 What a comfort to know that Jesus was praying for *us* and that He wants to share with us the glory of God (verse 22).

From verses 23 on, what does He say that lets us know that we'll never really be alone again if we believe and trust in Jesus.

Prayer Suggestion

Remembering that Jesus wants us to be one with Him and the Father and that He even wants us to share His glory—pray that we might really *know* what this means in our lives and that we might have a real *hunger* to prayerfully study His Word.

JESUS PRAYS FOR HIS FOLLOWERS—JOHN 17:11–26

37A

Opening Prayer (Father)

Heavenly Father, guide us as we study Your Word. Help us to understand Your message to us, and teach us how to apply it in our lives, in Jesus' Name. *Amen.*

Scripture Reading (Mother)

Others follow in their Bibles.

Questions (Mother)

FOR CHILD	1	To whom is Jesus talking?
FOR TEEN-AGER	1	What does Jesus want for His followers and ask God to do for them in these verses (11, 13, 15, 17, 21, and 24)?
FOR ADULT	1	Read verse 20 and put it in your own words.
	2	What does Jesus say He will continue to do for His followers?

Closing Prayer (Teen-ager)

Thank You God for the great love Jesus shows for His disciples and for us which we read about in this passage. Thank You for all You have done for us through Jesus Christ, Your Son. *Amen.*

JESUS' ARREST—JOHN 18:1–14

38

Prayer

Introduction

Jesus' Last Supper, eaten with His disciples in an upper room in a house in Jerusalem, was now over. Jesus had spent time teaching and praying with these dear friends.

If you have extra time, try reading Luke 22:39–53 for additional details.

Read Scripture

Questions

1 Where did Jesus' little band head?
2 Describe Judas's activities. What did this show of his character? (Also Matthew 26:47–50; 27:3–5; Mark 14:21.)
3 Consider Jesus' behavior in this difficult situation. How did He conduct Himself before the band of ruffians who came to arrest Him? How did He provide for the disciples (v. 8) and the injured slave? (Luke 22:51.)
4 Where did the Roman soldiers and Jewish officers take Jesus?

Suggested Hymn

"Go to Dark Gethsemane," p. 119, *Great Hymns of the Faith;* " 'Tis Midnight—and on Olive's Brow," p. 411, *Inspiring Hymns.*

Prayer

TEMPLE TRIAL AND PETER'S DENIAL— JOHN 18:12–27

39

Prayer

Introduction

Although Annas had been deposed from his position of high priest by the Roman ruler preceding Pontius Pilate, he still retained the title and even the controlling power. He was able to work through Caiaphas, his son-in-law.

Read Scripture

Questions

1 Name the people present at the informal hearing of Jesus' case before Annas. "Another disciple" is most likely a polite way of the author, John, referring to himself. Under Jewish law, trial before the Sanhedrin during the night hours was strictly forbidden and considered illegal.
2 What was Peter's special problem (*see* John 13:37, 38)? How do you think he felt after his third denial?
3 How did Jesus conduct Himself before these Jewish religious leaders?

Suggested Hymn

"Hallelujah, What a Savior!" p. 127, *Great Hymns of the Faith;* p. 302, *Inspiring Hymns.*

Prayer

JESUS' CIVIL TRIAL (PART 1)—JOHN 18:28–40

40

Prayer

Read Scripture

Questions

1 (vs. 28–32) Pilate with the Jews

Why was it necessary for the Jews to bring Jesus before Pilate, the Roman governor (v. 31)? Why couldn't they enter the praetorium (v. 28)? What time of day was it? How much was accomplished with Pilate outside the praetorium (v. 28)?

2 (vs. 33–38) Pilate with Jesus

Inside the praetorium, Pilate interrogated Jesus privately. His first question (v. 33) was a perfunctory one, based on the charges placed against Jesus by the Jews. What was Jesus' purpose in answering with yet another question?

In Pilate's second question (v. 35a), he was not seeking an answer. What attitude did it reflect?

His third question (v. 35b) required an answer and opened the door for Jesus to explain His position. How could Jesus' answer have reassured Pilate?

The fourth question (v. 37) was almost like a musing over Jesus' comments. How did Jesus explain His life-purpose (v. 37)?

His fifth and last question was really only a sarcastic or perhaps perplexed remark (v. 38).

3 (vs. 38–40) How did Pilate try to dispense with this annoying trial that had disturbed his sleep?

Suggested Hymn

"What Will You Do With Jesus?" p. 111, *Great Hymns of the Faith.*

Prayer

JESUS' CIVIL TRIAL (PART 2)—JOHN 19:1–16

41

Prayer

Introduction

A strange trial was in process at an unusually early hour (6 A.M. Roman time). Surely, Pilate would rather have been home enjoying his bed, but instead he had been called to the praetorium to bargain with a hostile group of Jews and an unnerving citizen named Jesus. Pilate had just declared his conviction of the prisoner's innocence and had tried to get the mob to settle for a compromise (18:38–40), all to no avail.

Read Scripture

Questions

1 What did Pilate try next, hoping to satisfy the Jews (v. 1)? How did the soldiers increase the indignities to Jesus (vs. 2, 3, 5)?

Roman scourging was considered part of the capital punishment. The victim was tied to a stake with his back bared to receive lashes from thongs weighted with jagged pieces of metal or bone. Prisoners often fainted and sometimes died from this procedure.

2 Describe the attitude and character of Pilate in all of this. Earlier in the trial, Jesus had answered his questions. In v. 9, Jesus remained silent. How did Pilate try to establish his authority over Jesus (v. 10)? What was Jesus' calm and majestic answer (v. 11)?

Suggested Hymn

"In the Hour of Trial," p. 88, *Inspiring Hymns.*

Prayer

THE CRUCIFIXION—JOHN 19:17–37

42

Prayer

Introduction

Although exhausted from a sleepless night and weakened by a severe beating, Jesus was assigned to carry His own cross to a place outside the city of Jerusalem.

Read Scripture

Questions

1 Name all the people present at the scene. Try to imagine how each one felt.

2 The activity of the godless, professional soldiers was a routine day's work for them, but it was a remarkable fulfillment of prophecy that they knew nothing about. (Psalms 22:18—The whole twenty-second Psalm pictures the Crucifixion scene.)

3 In spite of the agony of dying in such a gruesome way, Jesus had presence of mind and tenderness of heart to remember that dear woman who had borne Him and raised Him from infancy. The disciple mentioned here is the author of the Gospel of John. Why was it necessary to do this (7:3–5)?

4 God had long before described the death of His Son (*see* Psalms 69:21; 22). Jesus was careful to fulfill all that the Old Testament Scripture had said. When that was done, how did He die?

Suggested Hymn

"O Sacred Head Now Wounded," p. 116, *Great Hymns of the Faith;* p. 111, *Inspiring Hymns.*

Prayer of Thanksgiving

JESUS' BURIAL—JOHN 19:31–42

43

Prayer

Read Scripture

Questions

1 Why were the Jews in a hurry to clear the Crucifixion scene? Although they had their day of banqueting in mind, they actually ended up fulfilling prophecy (Psalms 34:20, Deuteronomy 21:23).

2 What is John's purpose in writing all these details (v. 35)? Have you ever realized that Jesus did this all for you, and then thanked Him.

3 Who came to claim the body of Jesus for burial (vs. 38–40)? What do you know about these men (John 3:1)? What must have prompted them to do this? Where did they put

His body? God had foretold that a rich man would make provision for Him in His death (Isaiah 53:9).

Suggested Hymn

"I Gave My Life for Thee," p. 375, *Great Hymns of the Faith;* p. 341, *Inspiring Hymns.*

Prayer

THE EMPTY TOMB AND THE LIVING LORD—JOHN 20:1–18

(The Revised Standard Version is used in this study.)

44

Prayer

Chapter 20 opens early on Easter morning.

Read Scripture

John 20:1–10

Questions

1 John 20:1 What did Mary discover when she went to the tomb?

2 John 20:2 To whom did she tell her findings?

3 Who was "the other disciple, the one whom Jesus loved"? This disciple is the author of the Book of John, the son of Zebedee, and the brother of James. This is the same John to whom Jesus entrusted His mother Mary at the cross.

4 What did Peter and John see when they looked into the tomb?

5 John 20:8 What does this verse reveal to us?

6 John 20:9 Had the disciples expected Jesus to rise from the dead? The disciples went home and Mary was left in the garden.

Read

1 John 20:15 Who did Mary think Jesus was when He first spoke to her?

2 John 20:16 When did Mary recognize Jesus?

3 What did Jesus request of Mary?

Food for Thought

It is noted twice that each disciple saw the linen clothes lying in the empty tomb. Beside the empty tomb, what is so significant about these linen clothes? The precise position of the different clothes is noted. The isolated napkin which had been used on Jesus' head suggests that Jesus left the grave clothes without disturbing them. The empty tomb and the linen clothes convinced John that Jesus was the One who He said He was. Is it more difficult for us to believe today than it was for John?

Close With Prayer.

(Reference 1: *Everyone in the Bible* by William P. Barker, pp. 194, 195.)

(Reference 2: *The New Bible Commentary: Revised* by Guthrie, D., Motyer, J. A., Stibbs, A. M., Wiseman, D. J., editors, p. 965.)

JESUS' ANSWERS TO THE DISCIPLES— JOHN 20:19–23

(The Revised Standard Version is used in this study.)

45

Prayer

Read Scripture

Questions

1 John 20:19 Why did the disciples have the doors shut where they were?
2 The doors were shut and yet Jesus came and stood among them. Can you explain that?
3 How did Jesus greet them?
4 John 20:20 What did Jesus do when He came into the room?
5 How did the disciples react to His being there?
6 John 20:21 What did Jesus mean when He said to the disciples, "As the Father has sent me, even so I send you"? Send them where and to do what?
7 John 20:23 Does this verse give us a clue to the disciples' duties when Jesus said, "So I send you"?
8 John 20:22 What will enable the disciples to do the work of Christ?

Food for Thought

1 Have these verses and the previous study given us a glimpse of the Resurrection Body? Jesus left the grave clothes undisturbed. Did the stone have to be rolled away for Him to leave the tomb *or* to show that He was gone? Jesus came and stood among the disciples when the doors were shut. What a marvelous body with characteristics about which we can just wonder and yet anticipate.

2 How can the disciples have the authority to carry out John 20:23? In Luke 5:32, Jesus said, "I have not come to call the righteous, but sinners to repentance." In this study (John 20:21), He tells the disciples, "So I send you." Those, who repent of their sins before God, and believe in the Lord Jesus Christ, who paid for their sins on the cross, can be forgiven. To those people, the disciples can say, "Your sins are forgiven." Those who do not repent "retain" their sins. Luke 24:45–47 and Acts 10:43 reveal these same thoughts.

Close in Prayer.

THOMAS BELIEVES—JOHN 20:24–31

(The Revised Standard Version is used in this study.)

46

Open With Prayer

In the previous verses of John 20:19–23, Jesus appears to the disciples behind closed doors. Thomas, one of the Twelve, was not with them when Jesus came.

Read Scripture

Questions

1 John 20:25 What did the other disciples tell Thomas about Jesus?
2 What was Thomas's response?
3 John 20:26 Again eight days later, what happened?
4 John 20:27 What did Jesus say? What did He have Thomas do?
5 John 20:28 How did Thomas react to Jesus?
6 John 20:29 Thomas had to see and touch Jesus before he declared, "My Lord and my God!" What does Jesus have to say about those who have not seen and yet believe?
7 Who are all "those" that Jesus refers to?
8 John 20:30 What does John, who wrote this Book, reveal to us in this verse?
9 John 20:31 According to John, what is the purpose of this Book?

Food for Thought

1 Should we be critical of Thomas because the other disciples had seen the evidence he demanded before he would believe? Christ understood this about Thomas and appeared to him, too. Think of the depth of understanding and love

that Christ had for Thomas. Does Christ have His hand out to us today with the very same kind of love and understanding? Hebrews 13:8 tells us that "Jesus Christ is the same yesterday and today and for ever."

2 Recall Thomas's statement, "My Lord and my God!" Jesus had been Lord to Thomas before this. The disciples called Jesus, Lord. John 13:9 and John 14:5 are two examples. Not until that moment when Thomas said, "My Lord and my God!" had Jesus been God to Thomas. Do you think that our experience today is usually the other way around? Most of us have always believed in God and the Bible, and only when we ask Christ to come in and take over our lives does He become the Lord and Master of our lives.

3 In John 20:30, we learn that Jesus did many other signs or miracles that are not recorded. Read John 20:31 again. What is meant by "life in his name"? Do you feel that enough material is recorded in the Scriptures so that one may know for sure where one will spend eternity?

Close With Prayer.

FAITH—JOHN 20:19–31

46A

Prayer

Summary

It was Sunday evening of the same day that Jesus arose from the grave. Mary Magdalene had talked with Him earlier that day when He appeared to her near the tomb. Mary later reported to the disciples that Jesus had said He was going to ascend unto the Father.

Read Scripture

John 20:19–31

Questions

CHILDREN	What did Jesus show to His disciples?
	Were the disciples glad to see Jesus?
	Who wasn't so sure that Jesus was alive?
TEEN-AGERS	Why were the disciples behind closed doors?
	What message did Jesus have for them?
ADULTS	How did Jesus treat Thomas's doubting?
	What statement about belief did Jesus make?
	What was John's purpose in writing this book?

Discussion

Analyze the character of Thomas

MEMORIZE Verse 31 (optional).

Prayer

(Reference material on the Gospel of John: *The Gospel According to John* by G. Campbell Morgan; *Understanding the Gospel of John,* Matthew Henry.)

JESUS SHOWS HIMSELF TO THE DISCIPLES AT LAKE TIBERIAS—JOHN 21:1–14

47

Opening Prayer (Father)

(Prayer requests and answered prayers can be shared here.)

Almighty God, open our minds to discover what You are saying to us in this passage of the Bible about Jesus; may our study together be pleasing to You, in Jesus' Name. *Amen.*

Introduction (Father)

After Jesus was crucified and raised from the dead, He did not immediately go to be with His Father in heaven. First He showed Himself to many people. In this true story, He appears to seven of His disciples while they are fishing and then eats breakfast with them.

Reading the Scripture

John 21:1–14 (Father)

Others follow in their own Bibles. (Little children might enjoy paper and crayons to draw a picture about the story.)

Questions (Mother)

FOR CHILD
1 What were the disciples doing in their boat?
2 Who called to the disciples from the shore?

FOR TEEN-AGER
1 How many fish did the disciples catch before Jesus spoke to them?
2 What did Jesus call to them from the shore?
3 What was their response?
4 What happened when they cast their nets on the right side of the boat?

FOR ALL
1 Why do you think that the disciples decided to go fishing? When Jesus first called them, He told them, "Follow me and I will

make you become fishers of men" (Mark 1:17). Note that, in these verses of John 21:1–14, the disciples were not successful until Jesus came onto the scene and told them what to do. Jesus did not reprimand them for going fishing; He understood their situation and helped them to be successful.

2 Jesus even had food prepared for them, knowing that they would be hungry after working all night. Did you notice that Jesus asked them to contribute some of their fish for the meal (John 21:10)? Can we learn anything from that verse? Jesus already had fish and bread ready for them (John 21:9). Can we sit back and expect Christ to do everything for us without any effort on our part?

Drama (Optional)

Instead of questions, dramatize the story. Younger children like this. Father selects family members to play the different parts and reads the story while the players act it out.

Closing Prayer (Teen-ager)

Heavenly Father, thank You for this story about Jesus appearing to His disciples. Help us to obey our living Lord, in His Name. *Amen.*

JESUS TALKS TO PETER—JOHN 21:15–25

48

Prayer (Mother)

Our Father in Heaven, as we read and study this last passage in the Book of John, teach us by Your Holy Spirit what You want us to learn. Prepare us to read and hear Your Word. We pray in the Name of Jesus Christ. *Amen.*

Introduction (Teen-ager)

After Jesus had been raised from death, He appeared to seven disciples after they had been fishing unsuccessfully all night. When they cast their nets on the right side of their boat, as Jesus told them to do, they caught enough fish to fill the net. Then they ate the breakfast Jesus prepared for them on the shore. Following the meal, Jesus questions Peter and gives him some instructions in this passage. There is also reference to John.

Read Scripture

John 21:15–25 (Father)

Others follow in their own Bibles

Questions (Father)

FOR CHILD

1 Who is talking to Peter?

2 What did Jesus ask Peter?

FOR TEEN-AGER

1 How did Peter answer the Lord's questions?

2 How many times did Jesus ask Peter if he loved Him and how many times did Peter say he did? (Remember the three times Peter denied Jesus (John 18:15–27)?

FOR ADULT

1 What instructions does Jesus give Peter?

2 Who is that "other disciple, whom Jesus loved" in verse 26?

FOR ALL

Why do you think John wrote verses 24 and 25?

Discussion Question (optional)

In John 18:15–17 and 18:25–27, Peter denies Christ three times. Do you think that in the above verses of this lesson (21:15–17) Jesus is giving Peter three chances to prove that he does indeed love Him? What a relief it must have been to Peter to have finally said, "Lord, you know everything; you know that I love you" (John 21:17). Think back in your own life about how difficult it is to say, "I'm sorry." On the human level, communications open up again once the air is cleared with an apology. On the spiritual level, we can keep communications open if we do our part (1 John 1:9).

Prayer (Child)

Thank You God for these things John wrote down for us to read that tell us about Jesus. Help us to believe in Jesus, to love Him, and to follow Him, in the Name of Jesus. *Amen.*

Studies in The Acts of The Apostles

Just as Genesis is a book of beginnings, so is Acts: the beginning of the Christian Church, widespread apostolic miracles, persecution and martyrs, Gentile converts, Church organization, missions. Although the full title is The Acts of the Apostles, many have suggested that it would be more aptly named The Acts of the Holy Spirit. His name appears about seventy times in Acts which records the acts of the Holy Spirit working through men.

The author is generally considered to be Luke, "the beloved physician," who was a Gentile. He also wrote the Gospel which bears his name. About the same age as Paul, Luke was his constant companion for the last twenty years of Paul's life.

Acts was probably written around A.D. 63 while Paul was still under house arrest. It is considered not only one of the most interesting books of the Bible but strategically important, in that it bridges the Gospel accounts with the letters to the churches and individuals that follow. Knowing the stories of how the churches were born makes the Epistles come alive. It shows how the Gospel spread from Jerusalem out as far as Rome in Europe and Ethiopia on the continent of Africa. It also explains how the Gentile world received the Good News that so many Jews had spurned.

Some have described the relationship of the Book of Acts to all of Scripture by reminding us that it seems more apparent that God the

Father is most active in the Old Testament; God the Son active in the Gospels; and God the Spirit active in the Book of Acts.

There is lots of action in the Book of Acts. See if your family doesn't find it one of the most exciting in the Bible!

(NOTE: Because of the length of the Scripture passages studied in The Acts, some lessons may be longer than the usual fifteen minutes. You may want to spend two evenings on those studies. A chronological order of events and maps of Paul's journeys and one of the early churches are provided so that your family can follow the action.)

Dates in the Chronological Chart may be regarded as approximately correct within a year or two, one way or the other.

CHRONOLOGICAL CHART OF ACTS

Events	*Dates*
Ascension (1:9–11)	A.D. 30
Pentecost (2:1–41)	A.D. 30
Early church (2:42–6:7)	A.D. 30
First persecution (4:1–31)	A.D. 31
Second persecution (5:17–42)	A.D. 32
Third persecution— Stephen's martyrdom (6:8–8:4)	A.D. 35–36
Philip's ministry in Samaria and to the Ethiopian (8:5–40)	A.D. 36
Paul's conversion (9:1–21)	A.D. 37
Paul in Damascus, Jerusalem, Tarsus (9:22–30)	A.D. 39
Peter at Caesarea (10:1–11:18)	A.D. 41
Foundng of Gentile church at Antioch (11:19–24)	A.D. 41
Paul in Antioch (11:25–26)	A.D. 43
Martyrdom of James; Peter imprisoned (12:1–19)	A.D. 44
First missionary journey (13:1–14:28)	A.D. 45–47
Jerusalem council (15:1–29)	A.D. 50
Second missionary journey (15:36–18:22)	A.D. 51–54
Third missionary journey (18:23–21:19)	A.D. 54–58
Paul arrested in Jerusalem (21:20–23:22)	A.D. 58
Paul a prisoner at Caesarea (23:23–26:32)	A.D. 58–60
Paul's journey and arrival in Rome (27:1–28:31)	A.D. 60–61

Outline

From Jerusalem to All Judea, Ch. 1–7
To Samaria, Ch. 8
To the Gentiles, Ch. 9–12
To the End of the Earth, Ch. 13–28

ACTS 1:1–14

1

Prayer

Introduction

Luke begins his sequel to his life of Jesus as recorded in the Gospel of Luke. In the Gospel, Luke told about Jesus' life, death, and Resurrection. Now we read about the forty days following Jesus' Resurrection when He appeared to His disciples and gave them instructions. Then, while the disciples watched, He returned to heaven, leaving them to follow His orders on earth.

Read Scripture

Questions

CHILDREN

1 Why did Jesus tell His disciples to wait in Jerusalem (v. 4)?
2 Why does God give us power (v. 8)?
3 What happened to Jesus after His command to His disciples (v. 9)?
4 What was the message of the "men in white robes" (v. 11)?

TEENS

1 How did Jesus give His instructions to the disciples (v. 2)? How do you think He instructs us today?
2 What happened during the forty days between the Resurrection and Ascension of Jesus (v. 3)?
3 What was the Father's promise (vs. 4, 5)?
4 What did the disciples do after the Ascension (vs. 13, 14)?
5 Is there a command to obey in this passage?

ADULTS

1 What is the significance of "began to do" (KJV) in verse 1?
2 What was the disciples' question (v. 6)? Jesus' answer (vs. 7, 8)?
3 What was not given to the disciples (v. 7)? What was given to them (v. 8)?
4 What is taught about Christ in this passage? About the Holy Spirit? About God the Father?

What About Me?

What does a witness do? (Look up *witness* in the dictionary.)

Am I being a witness for Jesus in my part of the world—my neighborhood, my school, my office? Is the power of the Holy Spirit evident in my witnessing?

The question the disciples asked in verse 6 showed their limited view and already established idea about what they believed Christ would do. Do I sometimes pray this way—telling God what to do, rather than asking for His will?

Springboard (optional)

MEMORIZE Acts 1:8.

Prayer

Pray for a specific person to whom you believe God wants you to be a witness. Help the children to discover ways in which they can tell their friends about Jesus.

ACTS 1:15–26

2

Prayer

Pray for God's guidance in your lives with the same reality which the apostles experienced.

Introduction

After Jesus' Ascension, the believers had gathered together to select a new apostle. The disciples selected two candidates for the position, and after prayer, they cast lots to choose between them. The Holy Spirit had not yet come. Today, we can rely on His direction in making such choices.

Read Scripture

Questions

CHILDREN
1 How many followers of Jesus were present when Peter spoke (verse 15)?
2 What disciple of Jesus did they need to replace (verses 16, 17)?
3 What was the first thing the men did before deciding who should be the new apostle (verse 24)?

TEENS
1 Who prophesied in the Old Testament about Judas (verse 16)?
2 What was Judas's fate (verses 18, 19)?
3 What were the requirements for a person to replace Judas (verses 21, 22)?

ADULTS
1 What was the prophecy concerning Judas (verse 20)?
2 What was the disciples' belief concerning the Old Testament Scriptures (verse 16)?

3 Who were the two persons nominated to replace Judas (verse 23)? How did they choose between them (verses 24–26)?

What About Me?

In what areas do I need God's guidance right now? I pray that God will show me how to choose the right course of action.

The apostles had a real part in bringing about the fulfillment of prophecy. Am I helping to fulfill God's plans today? Do I share the Good News of Christ? Do I bring others into His kingdom?

Springboard (optional)

Look up Matthew's account of Judas's fate (Matthew 27:3–10). At first glance, Luke's account in Acts 1:18, 19 seems to be different from Matthew's account. However, we can harmonize them in this way. When Judas had returned the silver to the priests, they still considered it his money, and they purchased a potters' field with it in his name. Apply the truth of Numbers 32:23 to the life of Judas.

Review the names of the twelve apostles, or encourage your children to learn them.

Prayer

ACTS 2:1–13

3

Prayer

Pray that God will give you understanding of today's passage.

Introduction

The day of Pentecost was a Jewish holiday. It was celebrated fifty days after Passover. On this Pentecost day, the Holy Spirit came and filled the believers. This had been promised by Jesus (John 16:7–16). In the Old Testament, it is said that the Holy Spirit came *upon* people. Now, after Christ's death and Resurrection, the Holy Spirit comes to *live in* the believer. Pentecost was the beginning of this new way of the Spirit's working.

Read Scripture

Questions

CHILDREN

1 What sound did the people hear (v. 2)?

2 What did they see (v. 3)?

3 What filled each of them (v. 4)?

TEENS

1 How many of the Christians gathered there were filled with the Holy Spirit (v. 4)?

2 What was so unusual about these people speaking in other languages (v. 4)?
3 What did the Christians speak about in these foreign languages (v. 11)?

ADULTS
1 How did the filling with the Holy Spirit affect the believers (v. 4)?
2 What was the reaction of the Jews gathered in Jerusalem for the celebration of Pentecost (v. 6)?
3 How did some people explain the occurrences (v. 13)?

What About Me?

Have I believed in Christ and been filled with the Holy Spirit? Can others see Christ's life in me? Does my life show the fruits of the Spirit (Galatians 5:22, 23)?

Do I tell others about the wonderful works of God?

Springboard (optional)

Look up other instances when God used the sign of wind (John 3:8, Ezekiel 37:9–14), and of fire (Exodus 3:2). Write a newspaper account of the events of Pentecost.

If you can locate a map (in the back of your Bible), try to spot the different locations mentioned here. How far had the visitors in Jerusalem traveled to get to Palestine? Just think what exciting news they could spread when they went home after the feast days!

Suggested Hymn

"O Breath of Life" by Bessie Porter Head, Norman Johnson, p. 170 in *Great Hymns of the Faith;* p. 92 in *Worship and Service Hymnal.*

Prayer

Pray that each member of your family will daily give himself to the Holy Spirit to be controlled by Him.

ACTS 2:14–21

4

Prayer

Pray that your family members will be fit vessels through which the Holy Spirit can work effectively.

Introduction

Peter explains that the speaking in other languages by the believers is the fulfillment of Old Testament Scriptures. God has poured His Spirit into the believers. The ways in which the Holy Spirit uses a person may be different, but it is the same Holy Spirit who lives in each believer in Christ.

Read Scripture

Questions

CHILDREN
1 What prophet does Peter mention (v. 16)?
2 In the prophecy, what does God promise to give to men (vs. 17, 18)?
3 How can a person be saved (v. 21)?

TEENS
1 Did Peter stand alone to address the crowd (v. 14)?
2 Why does Peter say the people could not be drunk (v. 15)?
3 What other signs has God promised (vs. 19, 20)?

ADULTS
1 What results of the outpouring of the Holy Spirit are mentioned (vs. 17, 18)?
2 What will follow the signs of verses 19, 20?
3 What does it mean to "call upon the name of the Lord" (v. 21)?

What About Me?

When people make fun of a Christian, do I come to their defense? Can I explain God's working in my life?

Have I asked Christ to be my Saviour?

Springboard (optional)

MEMORIZE Acts 2:21.

Look up the prophecy in Joel quoted by Peter (Joel 2:28–32). Read the entire Book to see the prophecy in its context.

Prayer

Thank God for His salvation given to us through the Lord Jesus Christ.

ACTS 2:22–36

5

Prayer

Pray for the guidance of God's Holy Spirit as you study His Word.

Introduction

Peter wants to show his listeners that Jesus is the "Lord" he has just mentioned in verse 21. He quotes from a psalm of David in which David spoke of the coming Saviour. Peter's listeners knew well the fact of Christ's Resurrection. In verse 36, Peter clearly states the Lordship of Jesus Christ, proved by His Resurrection.

Read Scripture

Questions

CHILDREN 1 Did Jesus remain dead? Who raised Him up (v. 24)?

2 What had God promised to David about one of his descendants (v. 30)?

TEENS 1 What proof did God give that Jesus was His Son (v. 22)?

2 How do we know that David was not speaking about himself (v. 29)?

ADULTS 1 Who planned Jesus' death (v. 23)? Who carried it out (v. 23)?

2 What particular part of David's psalm related to Christ (vs. 25–28)?

What About Me?

Do I believe that Jesus is the Lord?

Can I explain to an unbeliever about the Good News of Christ's life, death and Resurrection?

Springboard (optional)

Practice telling the essential facts of the Gospel. Ask God to help you to share your faith with others.

Prayer

Thank God for His wonderful plan for our salvation in Christ.

ACTS 2:37–47

6

Prayer

Pray for understanding of the nature of early Christian fellowship.

Introduction

Peter's first recorded sermon in the Book of Acts had great effect. The early gathering of the believers was for food, fellowship, prayer, and worship. Their number grew daily.

Read Scripture

Questions

CHILDREN 1 What did Peter tell his listeners they must do (v. 38)?

2 How many persons accepted Christ that day (v. 41)?
3 What did the early Christians do when they met together (vs. 42, 46, 47)?

TEENS
1 What was the reaction of Peter's listeners (v. 37)?
2 Did they follow Peter's command (v. 41)?
3 How often did they meet for fellowship and to receive instruction (vs. 42, 46)?

ADULTS
1 Why did the new believers exhibit a sense of awe (v. 43)?
2 What did the new believers do with their possessions (vs. 44, 45)?
3 From the entire passage, what attitudes and actions characterized the early believers?

What About Me?

Am I eager to learn God's Word? Do I regularly meet with other believers for fellowship?

Do I share my possessions with others?

Could others describe me as daily praising God?

Springboard (optional)

Discuss the concept of communal living as practiced by the early believers. Should this be practiced today? What reasons may have prompted the early Christians to live in this manner?

Prayer

LAME MAN HEALED—ACTS 2:41–3:11

7

Prayer

Read Scripture

Questions

1 Can you describe the life-style of Jesus' followers? What did they lack? What did they have? How did their group grow?

2 In addition to giving the apostles the beautiful gift of explaining God's plan by the method of preaching (2:14–36), He showed His undoubted power with "many wonders and signs" (2:43).

This description of the lame man at the Temple is just one outstanding example.

a How severe a physical problem did this poor man have (3:2)?
b What expectation did the man have from Peter and John?
c Was he disappointed?
d How did the people respond?

Prayer

ACTS 3:1–16

8

Prayer

Read Scripture

Questions

Verses 1–8

1 It was the custom of the poor to come to this gate seeking gifts (usually money). The apostles had nothing of this kind to give as Peter says in verse 6, and apparently this man did not know who they were. What *did* Peter have to offer? What happened? What was the man's reaction? To whom did he give the glory?

2 How was Peter able to offer this gift?
From where did his authority come?

3 Is this authority and power available to all believers? (*See* I Corinthians 12:7.) What is the purpose of miracles (John 14:13)?

Verses 9–16

4 What was the people's reaction?

5 Seizing this opportunity, what does Peter say to the people who rejected Jesus?

6 In verse 12, Peter makes a strong point about John and himself. What is it?

7 Read verse 16. This is an important verse. (*See also* John 16:23, 24.) In whose name should we pray? Who intervenes for us at the throne of God?

Prayer

Close in prayer and, if you should desire, ask God to teach you more about the authority we have, as children of God, in the Name of Jesus. *Amen.*

ACTS 4:1–14

9

Prayer

Read Scripture

Verses 1–7

Questions

1 Why do you think the priests and the Sadducees (members of a Jewish religious sect) were in such opposition to the preaching of the apostles? What was it that they did not believe (v. 2)?

2 What was the reaction of the people who heard them preaching?

3 The council was aware that a miracle had been performed but by what means they were not sure. What were they implying by asking, "By what power or by what name did you do this?" (RSV). (Remember that according to Leviticus 20:27 anyone dealing with an unfamiliar spirit or demon would be put to death.) Therefore, what was the council hoping to prove?

4 (Read 9–14.) What made the difference here in Peter's boldness as compared to the time when he denied Christ (*see* v. 8)?

5 What does *salvation* mean and what does it mean to you personally (*see also* Romans 1:16)?

6 Where did the knowledge and wisdom of Peter and John come from? Must we be well educated or have great understanding in order to receive this gift?

7 What was it that made the council think that they had been with Jesus?

NOTE: It is interesting to see that, when Peter declared that this had been done in the name of Jesus, the council believed that this must be true otherwise the man would not have been healed. This was proof of a divine work.

Prayer

Ask Jesus to fill you with the same boldness that Peter had. Then thank God.

BOLDNESS OF PETER AND JOHN—ACTS 4:1–23

10

Prayer

Read Scripture

Questions

Verses 1–4 Who joined forces to oppose Peter and his friends? (The Sadducees were a group of religious-political aristocrats who often opposed the priests and Pharisees, the religious purists, and always were against Jesus.) What power did they have?

Verses 5–12 The next day there was a gathering of the same team that had put Jesus to death. What was their line of questioning? Why were they worried about authority?

As you read Peter's forthright answer (v. 8–12), what is the central theme of his message (v. 10)? If you were one of the questioners how might you react?

Verses 13–23 What was the strategy of the council members? What do you learn about Peter and John (Luke 22:61, 62; John 20:19)?

What great change had taken place in these men?

Prayer

ACTS 4:15–31

11

Prayer

Read Scripture

Verses 15–22

Questions

1 What was the reaction of the council? Consider what is happening among the Jewish leaders today as many of their people are accepting Christ as the Messiah.

2 According to verse 19, who should we be obedient to first, God or man?

3 We have talked about the "reaction" of the council; however, what was their decision? Why? What was happening to the people?

4 (Read verses 23–31.) Notice verse 24. The church obviously must have been prayerfully supporting Peter and John and were overjoyed at their Good News. In this verse and in Acts 1:14, we read of praying in "one accord" or being

"united" (LB) in prayer. What does this mean? (*See* Matthew 18; 19; 20 and also Acts 4:32.)

5 Are verses 25–28 part of their prayer stating Old Testament prophecy being fulfilled? What are some of the classes of people who were against Christ?

6 What was their prayer request and how was it answered (vs. 29–31)? How does this apply to us?

Prayer

Remember the believers had already been filled with the Holy Spirit in chapter 2 but here they were praying for renewed power and boldness. May this be our closing prayer.

ACTS 4:32–37; 5:1–11

12

Prayer

Read Scripture

Acts 4:32–37

Here we have another example of a body of believers united in one spirit.

Questions

1 Discuss this and what it means to you and to your church.

2 In verse 33, what are they still preaching in spite of the command telling them not to (the command given by the council)? Why is the Resurrection so important?

(1 Corinthians 15:1–22 teaches the importance of the Resurrection.)

3 Why do you suppose there was such a spirit of unselfishness?

4 (Read 5:1–11.) What was it that Ananias and Sapphira conspired to do? Who did they lie against?

5 This was the first sin mentioned in the early Church. What were the results?

6 Discuss verse 4. Did anyone demand that they give all or part of their property, or was it theirs to do as they wanted? What, then, was the sin?

7 Why do you think the punishment was so severe?

NOTE: Keep in mind that at this time the Christian Church was just beginning. Those who claimed to be a part of it had a responsibility to set an example. What they did would have been very damaging to the testimony of the Church.

Prayer

Remember Proverbs 3:5—"Trust in the Lord with all thine heart; and lean not unto thine own understanding"!

ACTS 5:17–29

13

Prayer

Begin with a prayer that the Holy Spirit open up the Scripture and discussion.

Introduction

To set the stage for today's lesson, we find the apostles doing many miracles. The sick and demon-possessed were brought from all the towns around Jerusalem and all were healed.

Read Scripture

To be read from the Living Bible or Living New Testament (if at all possible).

(If you have younger children in your family who enjoy acting out stories, this would be a good way to bring this Scripture to life.)

Questions

1. When the High Priest had the apostles arrested, he thought they were his prisoners, but, by the way the story unfolds, we find they really weren't. Whose prisoners were they then? Notice that in Ephesians 3:1 (KJV) the Apostle Paul calls himself "the prisoner of Jesus Christ."
2. Try for a minute to put yourself in the apostles' place in jail. It's always easy to see God in the good things that happen to us, but what about the bad? Is He still in control? (*See* Romans 8:28; 1 Thessalonians 5:18.)
3. If you really realized that God is in control of the bad situations in your life, as well as the good, how would this change the way you would react to a problem? Discuss.
4. Can you think of a specific situation in your life where *knowing* this would make a difference?
5. Look at verse 29 again. Give an example in your own life when you might have to "obey God rather than men" (or even your friends). Discuss.

Prayer

It isn't easy to be thankful in all situations and it isn't easy to always "obey God rather than men," but our God is a powerful

God who wants to take us in our weaknesses and make us strong.

Let's ask Him right now to continue to change us into His likeness.

ACTS 5:30–42

14

Prayer

Begin with a prayer that the Holy Spirit open up the Scripture and discussion.

Read Scripture

Acts 5:30–32

To be read from the Living New Testament or Living Bible (if at all possible).

Questions

1 Notice the boldness with which Peter and the apostles speak about Jesus to the men who had just thrown them in jail. These are the same apostles who had run away in fear after Jesus was crucified. There must be something very different about these men now; what (or who) is the difference? Verse 32 gives a clue. (*See also* Acts 4:31.)

2 There are many times in our lives when we, too, need boldness to stand up for Jesus and what He wants us to do. Have you ever wanted to speak up for Him and found that the right words just wouldn't come out? Discuss.

We have a promise from Jesus concerning this very thing. (*See* Acts 1:8 and also Luke 11:9–13.)

Read Acts 5:33–42.

3 Have someone put in his own words the advice that Gamaliel gave to the council.

4 Was this good advice? Discuss.

5 According to verse 40, what were the apostles then told? The Scripture says we are to obey authority (Romans 13:1). Did they obey that order (*see* verse 42)? Why not (Acts 5:29)?

6 Why is this the one exception to obeying authority? Discuss.

Prayer Thoughts

In order to really "obey God," we must know what is in the Bible. Let's pray now that the Holy Spirit will give each of us a real hunger to learn His Word.

FIRST STRIFE IN THE EARLY CHURCH—ACTS 6:1–15

15

Prayer

Read Scripture

Acts 6:1–8

Questions

1 What was the Greeks' complaint against the Hebrews?

2 Do you think any large community can share all things in common for a long period of time without disagreement? Does this system seem practical?

Remember that this was not a command of the Gospel but of their own choosing. No one was forced to sell anything for the common good as proved by Acts 5:4. Usually this was a custom just during feast time when many people came to Jerusalem. Now people were staying longer because of all that was happening with the apostles.

3 What solution was offered by the disciples? What was the first priority of their ministry?

4 What were the qualifications for the seven men to be picked as business elders (v. 3)? Why do you think they specified men filled with the Holy Spirit? (*See* Acts 1:8.)

NOTE: Numbers 27:18–23 teaches the importance of laying on of hands for service.

5 What is the great miracle of verse 7?

6 Stephen was not one of the twelve apostles yet he also performed miracles in the Name of Jesus. Do all believers have this same power available to them? (*See* John 14:12.)

7 To what means did those of the synagogue resort to bring Stephen to trial (vs. 11, 13)? What was it that they couldn't come against?

Prayer

Praise God together.

STEPHEN—ACTS 6:1–15; 7:54–8:3

16

Prayer

Read Scripture

Questions

Acts 6:1–7 What problem had arisen between the Hebrews and the Hellenists (Greek-speaking people)? What does it show about their manner of living? Why couldn't the apostles handle this trouble?

Acts 6:8–15 Seven fine men were chosen. A cameo study of one in particular, is featured. Pick out the descriptive phrases that were soon to become his epitaph.

Who conspired against him and what were their charges?

If you have time, please read Stephen's magnificent sermon with its panoramic summary of Hebrew history.

Acts 7:54–8:3 How did the council react to Stephen's sermon? How did Stephen behave throughout this crisis? What important name appears at this execution scene?

Suggested Hymn

"A Mighty Fortress Is Our God," p. 36, *Great Hymns of the Faith;* p. 1, *Worship and Service Hymnal.*

Prayer

ACTS 7:2–19

17

Prayer

Begin with a prayer that the Holy Spirit open up the Scriptures and discussion.

Read Scripture

To be read in the Living Bible or Living New Testament (if at all possible).

Questions

1 Let's think for a minute about Abraham. What proves his great faith in God? (*See also* Hebrews 11:8–10.)
2 What does "faith" mean to you? Discuss.
3 Can you think of a time when you "believed God" and accepted one of His promises as your own?
4 Sometimes we think of faith only in terms of God, but faith operates in our lives in a small way every time we sit on a chair, lie on a bed, and so forth. What are you putting your faith in when you sit on a chair?
5 Just as we trust the chair to hold us up so we can *rest* into it, so it is when we trust (or have faith) in the promises of God. Every time you sit down into a chair do you worry whether it will really hold you up? What about God's promises? Should we worry whether He means it when He says, "I will never, never fail you nor forsake you" (Hebrews 13:5 LB)?

6 Is it always *easy* to trust God? Discuss. Why then must we put our faith in God's promise and not our *feelings* or doubts about His promise?

Prayer Thoughts

The Bible says that faith is a gift. Let's ask God right now to give us the faith to trust Him more. Do we dare to *claim* that promise for our own?

ACTS 7:37–53

18

Prayer

Begin with a prayer that the Holy Spirit open up the Scripture and discussion.

Read Scripture

Acts 7:37–43 To be read in the Living Bible or Living New Testament (if at all possible).

Questions

1 Verse 38 describes Moses as the go-between or the mediator between the people of Israel and the angel of God. From verses 37 to 39, how does this also compare with Jesus?

2 In verse 40, we find them turning away from God. Did God force them back (*see* verse 42)? What did He do?

3 Does He force us to worship Him?

4 What does He want from us? Discuss. (Read Acts 7:44–53.)

5 From verses 48–50, what do we learn about the greatness of God?

6 How do we know from this that God doesn't just live in "church"?

When we become God's children (John 1:12), God sends His Holy Spirit to live inside us. According to 1 Corinthians 6:19, what does our body then become? (Other translations use the word *temple* instead of *home.*)

7 Verse 51 talks about resisting the Holy Spirit. How did they resist Him? How might we resist the Holy Spirit? Discuss.

Hymn Suggestion

"How Great Thou Art!" by Stuart K. Hine, *Worship in Song—* Nazarene Hymnal

Prayer Thoughts

Let's stop now to think of the greatness of God and that our God who is so great has chosen to make His home within us!

Oh, Lord, help us *not* to *resist* Your Spirit and *not* to go *our own way* as the children of Israel did.

ACTS 7:54–8:3

19

Prayer

Read Scripture

Stephen has been giving his defense before the council; now we see what happens when he finishes.

Questions

1 Why were the priests so enraged?
2 Considering what was about to happen to Stephen, do you have any thoughts as to why God revealed His glory to Stephen at this time?
3 In verse 59, we see prayer offered up to Jesus. How does this verse along with verses 55 and 56 offer proof of Jesus as part of the Trinity?
4 Who is Saul? What has Saul been doing to the Church (8:1, 3)? Do you know who he becomes? (We will be studying the story of his conversion in chapter 9.)
5 Who else spoke almost the same words as Stephen at death?
6 What effect does this story of Stephen have upon you?

Prayer

Join together in praising God by singing "To God Be the Glory," to Him.

> To God be the Glory—great things He hath done!
> So loved He the world that He gave us His Son,
> Who yielded His life an atonement for sin,
> And opened the Life-gate that all may go in.

ACTS 8:4–25

20

Prayer

Introduction

There is much to be covered and learned from these next two chapters; but keeping in mind that this is a family study, we will not get into the real depth of them in this lesson. Some of you may want to study them further on your own or even together. Some reference verses are provided.

Read Scripture

Acts 8:4–8

Questions

1 What was the message that Philip preached (verse 5)? (*See* Luke 4:33–36.) What was the reaction of the people to what they saw and heard? What would your reaction be?

Read Acts 8:9–13.

2 Who did the people say Simon was? Why? What does God's Word say about involvement with sorcery and magic? (*See* Deuteronomy 18:10–12.)

3 What was the difference between what Simon was doing and what Philip was doing (in the area of miraculous power)?

Read verses 14–17.

4 Why were Peter and John sent to Samaria? (*See* Acts 2:38 for the promise of the gift of the Holy Spirit.) Is it necessary to have someone lay hands upon them to receive the Holy Spirit? (Remember the first outpouring of the Holy Spirit at Pentecost. *See also* 10:44–48.)

Read verses 18–25.

5 What was Simon's foolish desire caused by (verse 22)? What does verse 22 indicate about Simon's fate?

6 Even though Simon believed the Gospel and stayed with Philip, he fell under temptation. What kind was it? What should be our motives in seeking God's power?

7 Simon knew, though, what to do when he sinned. What was it?

This is the answer for anyone who has experienced sinning and has been forgiven for the sin. "If we confess our sins, he is faithful and just to forgive us our sins . . ." (1 John 1:9 KJV).

Prayer

Pray together keeping this promise in mind.

Suggested Reading: *Demons, Demons, Demons* by John Newport.)

ACTS 8:26–40

21

Prayer

Read Scripture

Philip left a city-wide revival to go into the desert to witness to one soul.

Questions

1 What would your decision be if the Lord spoke to you in this way? Why?
2 Why do you think Philip went so willingly?
3 Read verse 28. Do you think that the eunuch's heart had already been prepared by the Holy Spirit to receive the Good News?
4 What does this verse say that might lead you to believe this to be true?
5 To what are verses 32 and 33 referring?
6 Did Philip confine his explanation and teaching only to this portion of Scripture in Isaiah (v. 35)?
7 According to verses 36 and 37, what are the conditions for one to be baptized?
8 This portion of Scripture is a good example of personal witnessing and its victorious effect when led by the Holy Spirit. Can you name some of the things Philip did that we should also be doing in being faithful witnesses for Christ?

Prayer

Share prayer requests and answers to prayer together.

ACTS 9:1–19

22

Prayer

Introduction

Saul, the persecutor, wanted to find and kill all the followers of "The Way." ("The Way" was a name used by early Christians to describe their faith. Christ had said, "I am the Way," and they were His followers.) Saul's letter from the high priest also had the authority of the Roman government. But God had other plans —for Saul and for the followers of the Way.

Read Scripture

Questions

1 What happened to Saul on his way to Damascus? What was Saul's immediate response?
2 Why do you suppose he was blinded? (Read Paul's account of what happened in Acts 22:6–11.) It was during these three days that he became awakened to the fact of his sin and, in his zeal for God, had actually been fighting against Him.

3 (Read Acts 9:10–19, and also Acts 22:12–16 for same account.) What is a vision?
4 How did Ananias feel about this command at first (verse 13)?
5 True or false: According to verse 15 and Ephesians 3:7, 8, Paul was chosen to take the message to the Jewish people.
6 Discuss verse 16. How is this a reversal of Paul's former role?
7 What three things happened to Paul after Ananias went to him (verses 17, 18). Here is an example of the Holy Spirit being imparted through an ordinary believer.

What About Me?

Let each family member, who wants to, share his recollection of how he met Christ. Did God already have a purpose in His mind for me before I knew Him? Have I found and fulfilled that purpose?

Am I as obedient to God as Ananias who obeyed even though he was afraid? What things does God want me to do that cause me to be afraid? Had God prepared the way for Ananias? Will God prepare the way for me?

Springboard (optional)

Review the passage and notice particularly the characteristics of God's dealings with Saul and Ananias. Reflect on God's dealings with you.

Refer to Acts 22:1–16 and Acts 26:1–23 for Paul's own account of his conversion.

Prayer

ACTS 9:20–31

23

Prayer

Read Scripture

Questions

1 Why were the Jews amazed? What did they attempt to do to him? What happened?
2 Discuss verse 26. What would your reaction be to someone with a background like Paul's?
3 How was Paul able to speak with such boldness?
4 How did the believers help him?

5 What does it mean to walk in the "fear of the Lord" and "comfort of the Holy Spirit"? What are the results of this type of walk with the Lord?

Prayer

Praise God for the conversion of Paul and, as you close in prayer, keep in mind those for whom there seems to be no hope and remember Paul! God bless you.

PETER HEALS AENEAS AND DORCAS—ACTS 9:32–43

24

Prayer

Read Scripture

Questions

Verses 32–35 Aeneas

1 Who is the principal character in this account? What were Peter's activities?

2 What was Aeneas's problem? By what authority was Peter able to help him?

3 Although there was already a community of Christians at Lydda, what resulted from this miracle of healing?

Verses 36–43 Dorcas

4 On the map of Palestine (in New Testament times), find Lydda and then Joppa, both in the province of Judea. Try to picture the ancient walled city of Joppa built on a rocky ledge, overlooking the beautiful blue Mediterranean Sea.

5 Name the two prominent characters in this paragraph. Describe the problem that had arisen. From this brief account, describe the kind of person Dorcas had been.

6 Who demonstrated strong faith?

Once again a miraculous sign resulted in many turning to the Lord.

Suggested Hymn

"The Great Physician Now Is Here," p. 59, *Great Hymns of the Faith.*

Prayer

PETER AND CORNELIUS—ACTS 10:1–23

25

Prayer

Read Scripture

This next incident also took place in a town on the Mediterranean Seacoast. Find Caesarea, north of Joppa.

Questions

1 Describe the kind of person Cornelius was before he ever had contact with Peter. Wasn't he good enough? God knew something was lacking or He would never have gone to such particular trouble to teach Cornelius something new. Discuss.

2 Compare the call of Peter by Cornelius (10:5), with the call by Dorcas's friends (9:38). Why do you think God used such unusual methods (chapter 10:28) to bring Cornelius and Peter together? What is the outstanding character trait of both of these men? Whenever God spoke to them, what did they do? When you understand God's commands to you, are you quick to obey?

Suggested Hymns

"Where He Leads Me I Will Follow," p. 384, *Great Hymns of the Faith;* p. 200, *Inspiring Hymns;* and "I Have Decided to Follow Jesus," p. 397, *Great Hymns of the Faith.*

Prayer

PETER AND CORNELIUS—ACTS 10:23–48

26

Prayer

Read Scripture

Questions

1 What preparations had Cornelius made for the arrival of Peter (verses 24, 33)? What was his attitude toward Peter (v. 25)? Wasn't this a logical reaction (*see* v. 3)? How did Peter correct him (v. 26)?

2 Peter was the teacher, but do you know what new thing Peter himself needed to learn (v. 34)? What was the point of Peter's unusual vision (v. 28)?

3 When Peter "opened his mouth," he began to share the very Good News of peace. How did he bring them up-to-date on all that God had done? How does Peter claim the right to speak authoritatively (vs. 39, 41, 42)? What do you learn of God the Father (vs. 38, 40–42), Jesus the Son, and the Holy Spirit (vs. 38, 44) from this little home-delivered sermon? What is the important conclusion that Peter draws (v. 43)?

4 How did this episode affect the Hebrew Christians and the Gentiles who heard? How did God show how very much He approved of it all (v. 44)?

Suggested Hymn

"My Faith Has Found a Resting Place," p. 228, *Great Hymns of the Faith.*

Prayer

ACTS 12:1–17

27

Prayer

Introduction

The king we meet in this chapter is Herod Agrippa, grandson of Herod the Great, who was ruler when Christ was born. Herod Agrippa was liked by the Jews. He hoped to keep their favor by persecuting the Christians. Herod planned to kill Peter, as he had James, after the holiday of Passover. But God had other plans for Peter. The fact that James died, but Peter escaped is a mystery of God's working that we cannot understand.

Read Scripture

Questions

CHILDREN

1 Who was the king who arrested Peter (vs. 1–3)?

2 What did the people of the church do while Peter was in prison (v. 5)?

3 Who freed Peter from prison (v. 7)?

TEENS

1 Why did Herod arrest Peter (v. 3)?

2 What did Peter think of the angel's appearance (v. 9)?

3 Where did Peter go after the angel released him from prison (v. 12)?

ADULTS

1 When did Peter's miraculous release occur (v. 6)?

2 What were the angel's instructions (vs. 7, 8)? What was the result of Peter's obedience (v. 9)?

3 How did the believers first react to the news of Peter's release (v. 15)?

What About Me?

What does this passage teach me about prayer? About the timing of God's answers? About the methods God uses in answering? About requirements for answered prayer?

Discuss some recent answers to prayer in your family's life.

What do I obey—instructions received from God, as Peter did, or the whim of the people, as Herod did?

Am I sometimes surprised when God answers my prayer?

Springboard (optional)

Encourage the children to dramatize this story.

Make a further study on the subject of angels in the Bible. Some references are: Psalms 8:5; 91:11; 148:2; Daniel 3:28; 6:22; Matthew 1:20; 4:11; 18:10; 26:53; 28:2; Mark 12:25; Colossians 2:18; 1 Thessalonians 4:16; 2 Peter 2:4; Hebrews 1:13, 14; Revelation 10:1.

Prayer

(For further study: *Angels, Angels, Angels* by Landrum P. Leavell; "The Study of Angelology," *New "Panorama" Bible Study Course No. 2* by Alfred Thompson Eade.)

PAUL'S FIRST MISSIONARY TRIP STARTED—ACTS 13:1–14

28

Prayer

Introduction

Verses 1–3 Although there were actually sixteen Antiochs in the world of that day, all named in honor of the conquering founder Seleucus Nicator's father, Antiochus, the city mentioned here is Antioch in Syria. It was the third largest city in the Roman Empire (after Rome and Alexandria), with a population of about 500,000. Caravan routes from the East converged on this thriving commercial city, which was connected by a navigable river to the Mediterranean port city of Seleucia.

Read Scripture

Questions

Verses 1–3

1 There was already a Gentile church established. List the men here named and tell what their gifts were. What were they doing and what did God ask of them?

Verses 4–14

2 Who sent this little missionary team on its way? Look at the maps showing Paul's missionary journeys and trace the stops he made.

3 Where did they head first at Salamis? Who was already there to assist them?

4 Give a descriptive sketch of Elymas (Bar-Jesus) and of Sergius Paulus. What happened to the proconsul? What was the problem, and how did Saul (Paul) handle it?

5 Who left the fellowship of the missionaries to return to Jerusalem?

Suggested Hymn

"Anywhere With Jesus," p. 422, *Great Hymns of the Faith;* p. 23, *Inspiring Hymns.*

Prayer

FIRST MISSIONARY TRIP (Continued)— ACTS 13:1–5, 13, 14, 44–49

29

Prayer

Introduction

Before Christ returned to heaven, He had told His apostles to preach the Gospel. He promised them the power in the Holy Spirit. Now we see the Holy Spirit at work. Missionary work had begun!

Read Scripture

Questions

CHILDREN

1 Who were the two men chosen by the Holy Spirit to be the first missionaries (v. 2)?

2 Where did Paul and Barnabas go to preach in each town (vs. 5, 14)?

3 Where did God's message spread (v. 49)?

TEENS

1 From what church were the first missionaries sent (v. 1)?

2 How did the leaders of the church show their approval of the sending of Barnabas and Paul (v. 3)?

3 Who opposed Paul and Barnabas? Why (vs. 33, 45)?

4 How did the Gentiles receive the Gospel (v. 48)?

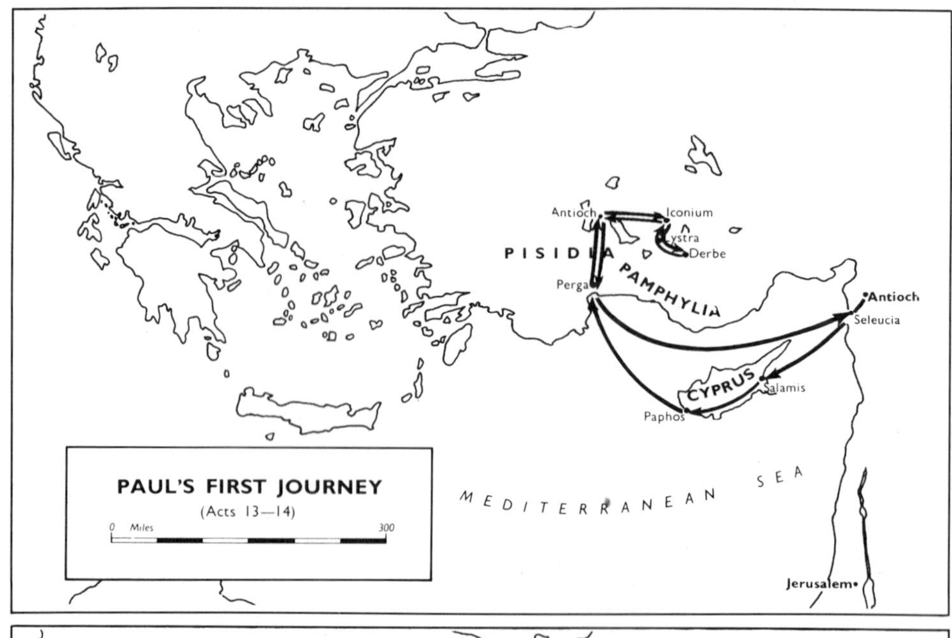
Antioch
Iconium
Lystra
Derbe
PISIDIA
PAMPHYLIA
Perga
Antioch
Seleucia
CYPRUS
Salamis
Paphos
MEDITERRANEAN SEA
Jerusalem
PAUL'S FIRST JOURNEY
(Acts 13—14)
0 Miles 300

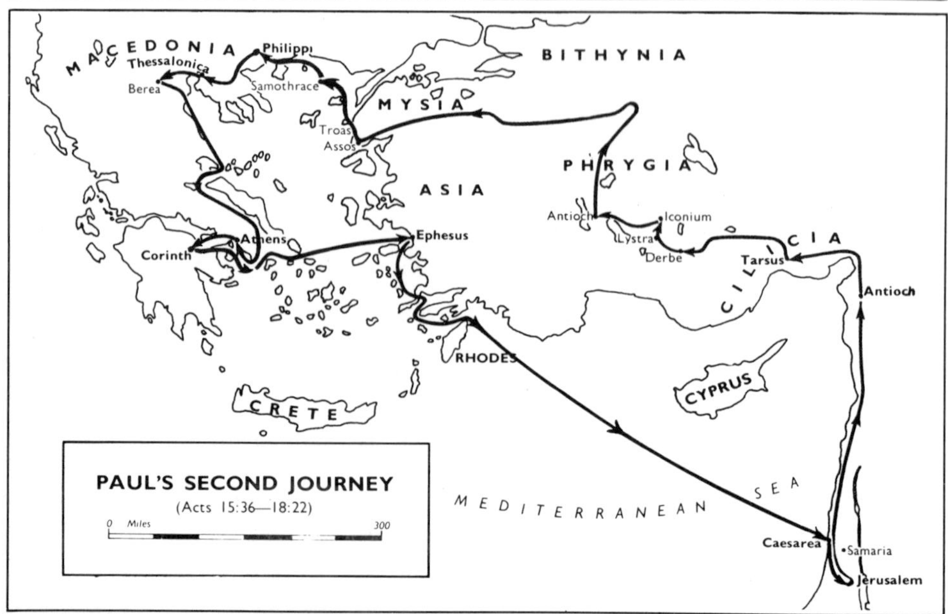
MACEDONIA
Philippi
Thessalonica
Berea
Samothrace
BITHYNIA
MYSIA
Troas
Assos
PHRYGIA
ASIA
Antioch
Iconium
Lystra
Derbe
Athens
Corinth
Ephesus
CILICIA
Tarsus
Antioch
RHODES
CYPRUS
CRETE
MEDITERRANEAN SEA
Caesarea
Samaria
Jerusalem
PAUL'S SECOND JOURNEY
(Acts 15:36—18:22)
0 Miles 300

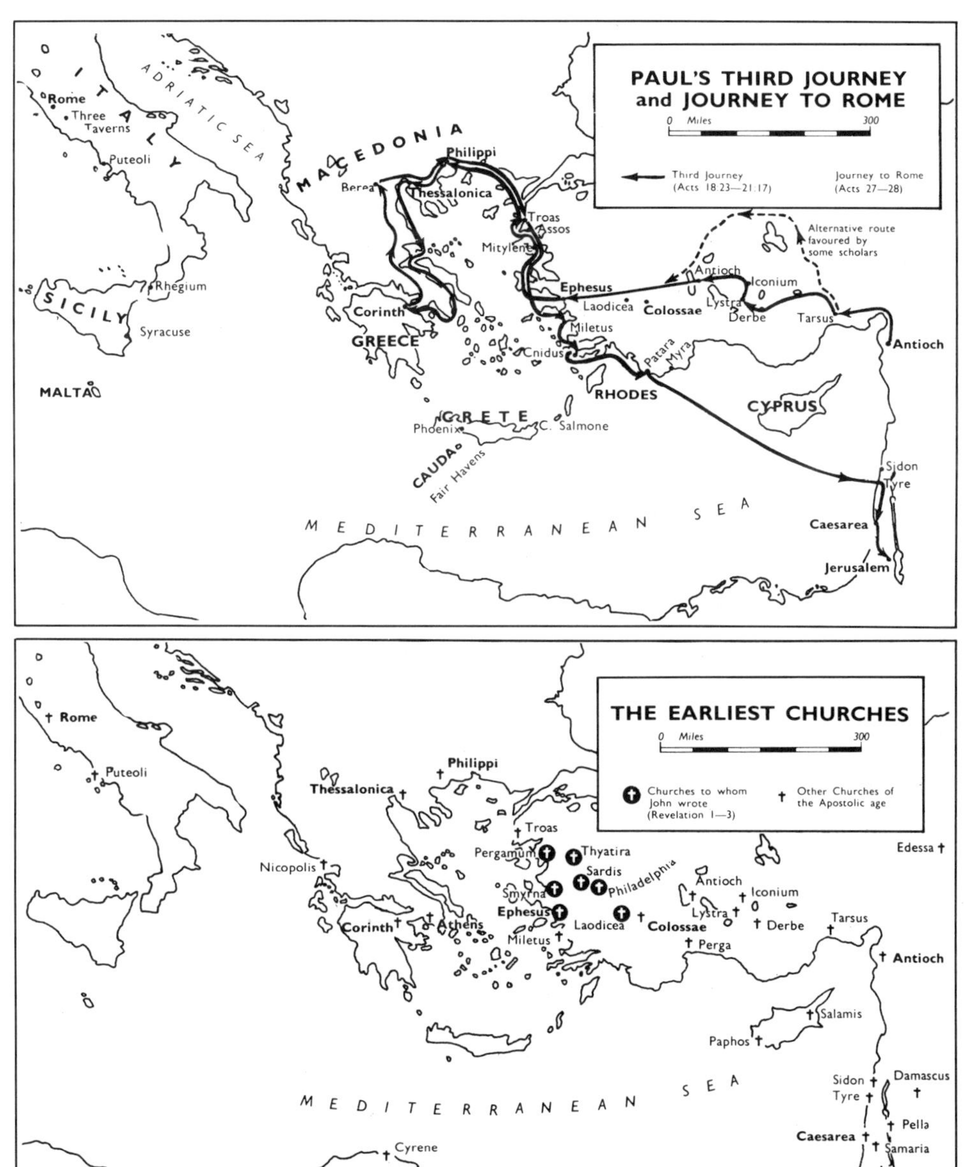
PAUL'S THIRD JOURNEY and JOURNEY TO ROME
0 Miles 300
Third Journey (Acts 18:23—21:17)
Journey to Rome (Acts 27—28)
Alternative route favoured by some scholars
ITALY
Rome
Three Taverns
Puteoli
ADRIATIC SEA
Rhegium
SICILY
Syracuse
MALTA
MACEDONIA
Philippi
Berea
Thessalonica
Troas
Assos
Mitylene
Corinth
GREECE
Ephesus
Laodicea
Colossae
Antioch
Iconium
Lystra
Derbe
Tarsus
Antioch
Miletus
Cnidus
Patara
Myra
RHODES
CYPRUS
CRETE
Phoenix
C. Salmone
CAUDA
Fair Havens
MEDITERRANEAN SEA
Sidon
Tyre
Caesarea
Jerusalem
THE EARLIEST CHURCHES
0 Miles 300
Churches to whom John wrote (Revelation 1—3)
Other Churches of the Apostolic age
Rome
Puteoli
Philippi
Thessalonica
Nicopolis
Troas
Pergamum
Thyatira
Sardis
Philadelphia
Smyrna
Ephesus
Laodicea
Colossae
Antioch
Iconium
Lystra
Derbe
Perga
Tarsus
Edessa
Corinth
Athens
Miletus
Antioch
Salamis
Paphos
MEDITERRANEAN SEA
Sidon
Tyre
Damascus
Pella
Caesarea
Samaria
Jerusalem
Cyrene
Alexandria

ADULTS

1 When did the Holy Spirit speak to the church leaders in Antioch (v. 2)?
2 Who directed Paul and Barnabas in their travels, methods, and effected results (vs. 4, 47, 48)?
3 What historic decision concerning the Gospel was stated by the men in verses 46, 47?
4 Who believed the Gospel (v. 48)?

What About Me?

Does the Holy Spirit direct me? Do I obey? Is the Holy Spirit working in the lives of other people through me?

When I hear God's Word preached, how do I respond? The Gentiles who heard Paul and Barnabas "were delighted and thanked God for his message" (Acts 13:48 PHILLIPS).

Springboard (optional)

Trace the travels of Paul and Barnabas on the map.

What did Christ teach about fasting (Matthew 6:16–18; 9:14, 15)?

What was the early church practice in regard to fasting (Acts 13:2, 3; 14:23)?

Make a missionary map noting missionaries supported by your church or known to your family.

Suggested Hymn

"Great Is Thy Faithfulness," p. 40, *Great Hymns of the Faith;* p. 403, *Inspiring Hymns.*

Prayer

Pray for faithfulness in the face of opposition.

PERSECUTION AND A MIRACLE—ACTS 14:1–10

30

Prayer

Loving Heavenly Father, we thank You for the Good News about Jesus Christ. May we let Him be Lord of our lives, just like Paul and Barnabas. Fill us with the Holy Spirit who will show us what You want us to know from this part of Your Book. Thank You! *Amen.*

Introduction

Paul and Barnabas have come from Antioch in Pisidia where the Gospel of Jesus Christ was rejected by the Jews and accepted by many Gentiles. The city leaders of Antioch were goaded by jealous Jews to persecute Paul and Barnabas who then went on to Iconium which is Gentile territory.

Read Scripture

Questions

Acts 14:1, 2

AGES 3–8 A To what building did Paul and Barnabas go? What is a synagogue? Who believed what they preached?

AGES 9–14 B Who made trouble by getting the Gentiles stirred up against the believers? How can someone make you believe what he is saying is true? How can a person poison another's mind?

ADULT C What are the three reactions to Paul's and Barnabas's message? Who are in each group?

Acts 14:3

A What did God do to show He approved of what Paul and Barnabas said and did?

B What was the reaction of Paul and Barnabas to the fact that many were against them? Do you think that they reacted this way because they knew they were speaking "for the Lord"?

C Briefly tell from where the power for miracles and signs comes and what Paul and Barnabas have done before these take place. For what reason did the signs and miracles occur?

Acts 14:4–7

A Were many people against Paul and Barnabas?

B Are there any people in Iconium on the apostles' side? Who were they and why?

C Paul and Barnabas leave when they hear the threats against their lives, but do they stop preaching? How might this be an example for us when we are witnessing?

Acts 14:9, 10

A If a man were crippled from the time he was born, would he have any leg muscles or know how to balance if suddenly his feet were healed? When Paul tells him to stand, does he say he can't? What does he do?

B When Paul first meets this man, what does he do while Paul is speaking? In Luke 8:8 (RSV) Jesus says, "He who has ears to hear, let him hear." (PHILLIPS translation says "use them.") Do you listen and really hear (Romans 10:17)?

C In the Amplified Bible, James 2:17 says, "So also faith if it does not have works (deeds and actions of obedience to back it up), by itself is destitute of power—inoperative, dead." What two actions show this man's faith? Do you have an active faith in what God has said in His Word about your present problems? If so, share it. If not, confess it, and see God lead you to action.

Prayer

Ask the Lord to show us what we are not hearing, our faithlessness, and our lack of action.

PAGAN REACTION TO THE MIRACLE AT LYSTRA—ACTS 14:11–23

31

Prayer

Introduction

Paul and Barnabas in Lystra have just caused the cripple from birth to walk.

Read Scripture

Questions

Acts 14:11, 12

AGES 3–8 A Who did the Lycaonians think Paul and Barnabas were?

AGES 9–14 B Whose gods were Jupiter and Mercury (also called Zeus and Hermes)?

ADULT C Today, when the supernatural happens, to whom does the modern man without Jesus Christ attribute the event?

Acts 14:13

A Whose priest came to offer sacrifices?

B If they had offered these sacrifices, who would get the glory?

C Why would the priest of Jupiter want to honor Paul and Barnabas? From this incident, would you conclude they knew their gods?

Acts 14:14–18

A Did Paul and Barnabas accept the honor of being called gods? Who did they want the people to know had healed the crippled man?

B When Paul and Barnabas said that they should turn to the living God, what did this say about the gods these people had been worshiping? What events did they say showed God's everyday kindness to these people even though they didn't recognize Him?

C Pick out the natural tendencies of mankind that are displayed by these Lycaonians. In your own words, what is the Good News Paul and Barnabas brought?

Acts 14:19

A Who came to speak against Paul? Were they from this city?

B Why did these men from Antioch and Iconium want to be rid of Paul?

C From being honored as gods to being stoned seems like a swift change of attitudes. What has Paul done? Does mob action often lead to incomprehensible acts? How?

Acts 14:20–23

A After Paul was thought dead, what happened when the believers stood around him? Would you have been surprised?

B Show on the map where Paul went after Lystra and Derbe. Why did he go there?

C How are Paul's actions an example for what he is telling the believers in Antioch, Lystra, and Derbe? The elders were appointed as human leaders, but to whom are they committed to be loyal?

Paul and Barnabas were on a mission to tell the Good News of Jesus Christ. As the Word of God is preached, God's power is shown, but men's rejection of the truth causes suffering for the preachers. Are you following their example?

Prayer

A MESSAGE TO THE GENTILE CHRISTIANS—ACTS 15:1–12

32

Prayer

Introduction

Paul and Barnabas have returned to Antioch in Syria, the starting place of their first missionary journey to the Gentile nations.

Read Scripture

Questions

Acts 15:1, 2

AGES 3–8 A Whose custom do the men from Judea want others to keep? Do you think these men from Judea are circumcised?

AGES 9–14 B In what province is Jerusalem (*see* map)? Why do Paul, Barnabas, and some of the Christians from Antioch go to Jerusalem?

ADULT C What is the real issue these men are trying to teach? Are you saved by an outward action (John 3:36)?

Acts 15:3–5

A Are the Christians in Phoenecia and Samaria glad that the Gentiles have been converted?

B Why would the believers from the Pharisee party think the Gentiles should be circumcised and keep the Law of Moses?

C Do you know any requirements that men through the ages have insisted others must meet to be saved? When Cornelius, a Gentile, heard Peter testify about Jesus and believed, did God say he should be circumcised (Acts 10:44–47)?

Acts 15:6–11

A Does Peter say God knows what everyone is thinking? What did God give to the Gentiles when they believed in Jesus?

B Why do you think Peter is the one to speak to the apostles and elders? Did Peter previously have to change his own thoughts about Gentiles when he spoke to Cornelius (Acts 10:34)? What does Peter say is the *only* reason he and those present are saved?

C Who does Peter say is being provoked by those Jews who are trying to make the Gentiles live as Jews do? What does Peter mean when he says that neither they nor their fathers could bear this yoke or burden (Romans 3:20; 1 John 1:8–10)?

Acts 15:12

A What did Paul and Barnabas tell about as soon as Peter finished?

B Who is responsible for these miracles? Why do you think Paul and Barnabas tell these events immediately following Peter's speech?

C Who is the only basis of salvation to both Jews and Gentiles? Who is the basis of signs and wonders? What part did Paul and Barnabas play?

Prayer

Lord, give us direction in controversy. Keep us from imposing our tradition on others of Your servants, while holding Your Word as the measuring stick of actions. *Amen.*

A MESSAGE TO THE GENTILE CHRISTIANS—ACTS 15:13–21, 36–41 (continued)

33

Prayer

Read Scripture

Questions

Acts 15:13–19

AGES 3–8 A James (Galatians 2:9) repeats a part of the Old Testament which is the Book of the Jewish religion. Are the Gentiles named in this Scripture? (*See* Amos 9:11, 12.) Do the reports of Paul and Barnabas agree with these words from the Old Testament Prophet Amos?

AGES 9–14 B What obstacles or troubles is James referring to in verse 19? What does he suggest they should tell the Gentiles?

ADULT C From James's statements, do you see whether he believes there is any question that many Gentiles have become believers and are saved? How does it appear that he has come to this conclusion? What example is here for us (John 5:39, Acts 17:11)?

Acts 15:20, 21

A Does James want to help the new Gentile believers? If you know an older person likes you and wants to help you, do you want to do what he tells you to do?

B What are the three instructions James suggests be sent to the Gentile believers? Considering what they had worshiped before they heard the Gospel, why do you think these instructions were sent?

C Does James give an indication that Gentiles should completely disregard the writings of Moses because they are now receiving instructions from the "home" church at Jerusalem? Some Christians take the attitude that since we are saved by faith alone that the law has been discounted. In Romans 7:6, 7; 8:1–4, Paul shows the proper perspective between law and grace. After reading this experience of the early Christians, briefly put in your own words how you would explain the law to a new believer in Jesus Christ.

Acts 15:36–41

A Why does Paul want to go back to the towns that he and Barnabas had visited? Who is Paul's assistant now? Who is Barnabas's assistant?

B Why doesn't Paul want to take John Mark? Barnabas means Son of Comfort. What personality would this indicate to you? Give an example how God has used different types of people for different jobs.

C Paul and Silas have had a successful missionary journey into Gentile territory and are now returning separately to visit. What words or phrases show that even though they succeeded on the first trip, their human abilities weren't sufficient? How can you use the actions of the believers who were with Paul at Antioch as an example of your duty to those who are preaching the Gospel today?

As experienced by the first believers in Jesus Christ as Lord and Saviour, there was disagreement because of background and tradition. We can profit in similar circumstances by their example: (1) that the first and only requirement for salvation is true faith in the Lord Jesus Christ, (2) that the Scriptures give us directions for actions, and (3) that other believers can instruct us in actions that can keep us in a productive and happy life for God.

Prayer

Pray for the Holy Spirit to direct in any controversial matter you are facing and to give you love for the other person even if you can't agree.

CHURCH MOVEMENT—A SLAVE GIRL SET FREE—ACTS 16:6–24

34

Prayer

Read Scripture

Questions

Acts 16:6–10 (Trace on the map the progress in this passage)

AGES 3–8 A What person of the Trinity is directing Paul and Silas? How does Paul know he should go to Macedonia?

AGES 9–14 B Did Paul and Silas obey the Holy Spirit's directions? How did Paul react to the vision?

ADULT C (optional) How can you test whether you are obeying the Holy Spirit's directions? (2 Timothy 2:15.)

Acts 16:11–13 (Continue to trace Paul's journey)

A What city in Macedonia did Paul and Silas visit? What gathering did they visit on the Jewish Sabbath?

B Since it was a Roman colony, did the population probably consist of more Jews or Gentiles? The Sabbath was whose day of worship?

C How do you think Paul and Silas knew to go to the riverside? To whom do you think these women were praying? (Remember the nationality and day of worship.)

Acts 16:14, 15

A Who opened Lydia's heart to believe Paul's message about Jesus? In whom did she already believe?

B What first action showed that she believed Paul's message? What does she say that convinces Paul that she is a true believer? What actions do you have that show that you really believe?

C Is there any admonition from Paul because Lydia is a business woman? What was the only important issue? To whom is Lydia responsible for her actions in daily living? To whom are we responsible? Can others see this by your life?

Acts 16:16–18

A Tell what "a spirit of divination" means or find out from someone in your family. Does the girl tell the truth about Paul and Silas?

B What was the relation between this girl and the men who received money from her fortune-telling? Whose name is used to make this spirit come out? Who only has the power?

C Why do you believe Paul commanded the spirit to come out when the truth was being told (Mark 1:24, 25)? Who is it that opens hearts (v. 14) and who was the power behind this girl's statement?

Acts 16:19–24

A Why were Paul and Silas accused before the rulers of the city? Did the rulers give them a fair trial?

B Had Paul and Silas done anything wrong? Under whose control were the slave girl's owners, the magistrates, and the crowds? Tell of some current event that has happened because the people involved were under the two different spiritual rulers.

C Scripture has always said to keep away from divination, astrology, and so forth (Deuteronomy 18:9–12). What example is set for our reaction to the many witches, astrological charts, fortune-tellers that are making their appearance today? Who alone has power over these spirits of darkness?

Prayer

Lord Jesus, help us to listen to You and let Your power keep us from the evil around us. *Amen.*

(For further study: There are a number of books available on the occult. *See* the Bibliography in the back of this book for suggested reading.)

PHILIPPI PRISON, PRAYER, PARDON, PRAISE—ACTS 16:25–40

35

Prayer

Read Scripture

Questions

Acts 16:25, 26

AGES 3–8 A Who heard Paul and Silas? Who has control over earthquakes?

AGES 9–14 B If you were a prisoner in the Philippi jail, describe at least three emotions you might feel at the events told in this Scripture.

ADULT C How do Paul's actions toward the jailer show us God's direction for treating those who mistreat us? Whose actions helped cause this man to call out in desperation, ". . . what must I do to be saved?"

Acts 16:31–34

A Does Paul tell the jailer he has to be kind and good to be saved?

B What actions now show that this man believes? Which came first, belief or action?

C Others were affected by this jailer's experience. How does he show his concern for those near him? Can you give an example from your experiences today of similar concern?

Acts 16:35–39

A Why don't Paul and Silas leave when the jailer says they are free? Who does Paul want to come to let them out?

B Paul, though a Jew, was born in a Roman-controlled city and therefore was a Roman citizen by birth. Why were the magistrates worried when they heard he was a Roman citizen? Had the officials given Paul an opportunity to defend himself?

C Why do you think Paul insisted the magistrates come in person? Do Paul and Silas prosecute these men? Who lived in this area and would know the whole story? Would this make it easier for the believers in Philippi?

Acts 16:40

A Did Paul leave the city right away? Whom did he go see?

B What did Paul's visit do for the believers in Philippi?

C Paul's concern for the new believers is shown. How can you, as a believer, actively or passively follow Paul's example?

The Good News of salvation has now spread to Europe. People from very different backgrounds and cultures have accepted Jesus Christ as Lord and Saviour.

Prayer

PAUL IN ATHENS—ACTS 17:16–34

36

Prayer

Introduction

Paul has been brought to Athens to keep him from those who wanted to harm him because of his message.

Read Scripture

Questions

Acts 17:16–18

AGES 3–8 A Why was Paul so disturbed in the city of Athens?

AGES 9–14 B With what four different groups of people did he discuss the religious situation?

ADULT C What was Paul's message? How did the philosophers react to this message? How do they try to discount what Paul is saying?

Acts 17:19–21

A What did the people of Athens like to do all the time?

B Do you think the men *really* wanted to listen to what Paul was saying?

C Jesus said the message (seed) would fall on different types of soil. What groups today are like these men of Athens when they also hear the Word?

Acts 17:22, 23

A Did the people of Athens worship more than one god? How many gods does Paul worship?

B What altar inscription does Paul use as the starting point in his message?

C What is the religious background of Athenians? Do they know the Scriptures like the Jews?

Acts 17:24–31

A What do the people think when they hear about Jesus' Resurrection? What do you think about Jesus' Resurrection from death to life?

B 2 Corinthians 2:15, 16. Paul says there are two reactions to his message. How are these two reactions shown by the people in Athens?

C How did you react when you first heard about Jesus and His Resurrection? Ask others in your group this question.

Conclusion

Paul is confronted in Athens with men who do not have the background of Scripture, but his message starts with their natural desire to worship a deity and goes on to the Resurrection of Jesus Christ. Only those who really seek truth come to believe, although there is a natural desire for knowledge.

Prayer

ACTS 18:1–23

37

Prayer

Begin with a prayer that the Holy Spirit open up the Scripture and discussion.

Read Scripture

To be read in The Living Bible, if possible.

Questions

1 How do we know from this that, although the Jews were His chosen people, God is looking for people to obey Him and if the Jews won't listen, He will find people who will? (*See* verse 6.)

Jesus gave His disciples instructions along these lines when He was on the earth. (*See* Matthew 10–14.)

2 What about us, if we harden *our* hearts against God, will He force us to obey Him?

3 See verses 9 and 10. What does this show us about God's power? What about Satan's power? Can Satan touch those

who belong to God without God's permission? (*See also* Job 1:12, 13 LB.)

4 In verse 23, we find Paul traveling from place to place visiting the believers. What does the Scripture say was his purpose in doing this?

5 Do we as believers need this, too? Why? Discuss.

6 Since we usually don't have someone like Paul traveling to our homes to strengthen us, how can we get the strengthening and encouragement we need today?

7 How can *you* strengthen and encourage someone else?

Prayer Thoughts

Realizing the importance of going to church, reading the Bible, and spending time with the Lord in prayer, let's ask Him now to give us a real desire for these things.

APOLLOS'S MINISTRY—ACTS 18:24–19:10

38

Prayer

Read Scripture

Make sure more than one translation is available.

Questions

Acts 18:24, 25

AGES 3–8 A Who does Apollos talk about?

AGES 9–14 B How would you describe Apollos?

ADULT C What type of modern person fits Apollos's description?

Acts 18:26–28

A Apollos knew the Scripture of that day, which was the Old Testament. Does he know Jesus as his own personal Saviour?

B What does the statement "the way of God more accurately" (RSV) or "the new way . . . in greater detail" (NEB) mean to you? (Priscilla and Aquila have been with Paul and believed his message.)

C What does "baptism of John" mean? Apollos knew the Scriptures and he was repentant, but what did he need to be saved? When he believes all the truth, how is he a help to the believers at Achaia? Is it enough to know the truth about Jesus without a personal commitment?

Acts 19:1–4

A About whom hadn't these disciples heard? Whose message had they heard?

B What was John the Baptist's message?
C Had these converts received the Holy Spirit? Did they want to? Why hadn't they received Him before?

Acts 19:5–7
A Whose name were these converts baptized into? Ask someone to read from a dictionary all the meanings of baptism.
B What is the sign that the Holy Spirit has come upon them?
C When a truth is presented, what must come before it changes the hearer?

Acts 19:8–10
A Paul was sent as a missionary to the Gentiles. Does he still try to witness to the Jews?
B Why does Paul move from the synagogue to the hall of Tyrannus?
C Why did Paul continue to witness in this hall? Show where Ephesus is and why this was carrying out his commission (Acts 9:15, 13:2, 3).

Conclusion

Paul is following the commands of the Lord to be a witness for Him; he sees the Lord save many and give signs of their belief. If you have believed in Jesus as Lord and Saviour, there should be some evidence of this belief. Is there?

Prayer

ACTS 19:1–20

39

Prayer

Begin with a prayer that the Holy Spirit open up the Scriptures and discussion.

Read Scripture

Acts 19:1–12 To be read in the Living Bible or Living New Testament (if at all possible).

From these verses, we learn much about the mighty working of the Holy Spirit on the earth.

Questions

1 Looking at verses 6, 8, 11, and 12, share what you learn about the power of the Holy Spirit within Paul.
2 In some places, the Scripture refers to the Holy Spirit as the Spirit of Jesus. Is this Mighty Power still on earth today? Discuss. (*See* Hebrews 13:8.)

Read

Acts 19:13–20

3 How do we know from these verses that the Name of Jesus is a mighty and powerful name and can't be fooled around with by those who don't belong to Him?

(*See* Mark 16:17 for the authority Jesus gave to those who did belong to Him.)

4 Reread verses 18 and 19. There is much of the occult, witchcraft, black magic, and the like going on among young people today. What do the words *confessed* and *burned them* tell us about what God thinks of these practices? Discuss.

5 Have you or any of your friends ever been asked to participate in any of these practices in the schoolyard, at slumber parties, and so forth?

6 Since these things do not operate by God's power, whose power must be behind them?

Prayer Thoughts

If you have ever been involved in any of these things, this would be a good time to "confess" and "burn" anything of this nature. The power of Jesus is here to cleanse and forgive. Let's ask God to show us the *power* of His Spirit so that we might not be satisfied with anything less.

PAUL VERSUS THE IDOL MAKERS—ACTS 19:23–20:1

40

Prayer

Introduction

Paul has been preaching the Word at Ephesus for almost two years and many have believed.

Read Scripture

Questions

Acts 19:23–27

AGES 3–8 A Who is the goddess that these silversmiths make images of? Why don't they like Paul?

AGES 9–14 B What is the real reason Demetrius wants to get rid of Paul? What does he do to get others on his side?

ADULT C What seems to be the most important thing to Demetrius? Read Matthew 16:26 and apply it to Demetrius and these idol makers.

Acts 19: 28–31

A How does a mob act? Do they stop to think if they are doing the right thing?

B Who was dragged into the theater? Why didn't Paul go?

C Why didn't the believers want Paul to go and speak at this time? Does this show distrust of the Lord's ability to protect His witnesses?

Acts 19:32–34

A Who tries to quiet the crowd? Would the crowd listen?

B What did the Ephesians have against Alexander? Who did the Jews (not the believers) worship?

C Trace the mob psychology that is exhibited here. What force is very evident?

Acts 19:35–41

A What does the town clerk say is the right way to bring a charge against anyone?

B The people have been yelling praise to Diana. How does this clerk tell them that they are doing something they really haven't thought about?

C How is this man's diplomacy shown in his speech? Did he really care for the men who were dragged into the theater? Who is he really concerned about? There is no indication that this man is a believer, but God used him to help the believers and the spread of Christianity. Do you know any examples of this in your community?

Acts 20:1

A When you have something unpleasant happen, do you like to talk it over with someone who you know has experienced the same situation but hasn't let it stop him from doing the right thing?

B How can we encourage Christians who have had hardships and trials?

C Discuss difficult experiences that you or your friends have had; but now, because you know the Lord, these trials help you to encourage others.

Our neighbors don't make idols to Diana or other gods, but material possessions have become idols to many. Is your witness to these neighbors showing that Jesus Christ is more important than anything else in your life?

Song Suggestion

"To God Be the Glory"

Prayer

ENCOURAGEMENTS AND EUTYCHUS—ACTS 20:2–12

41

Prayer

Read Scripture

Trace the route Paul follows from Macedonia to Troas (vs. 2–6).

Questions

Acts 20:2–6

AGES 3–8 A Why does Paul go back through cities he has preached in before?

AGES 9–14 B What group seems always to be against Paul and trying to get rid of him? What nationality was Paul and what religion was he before his conversion?

ADULT C (Mark 6:4) Jesus tells His disciples that those who preach God's Word will not be accepted by those who were close to him before he was saved. Paul's experiences show this. Do you know any examples in your family? Tell them. Who in this chapter (vs. 2–6) would be an encouragement to Paul?

Acts 20:7

A (Read Matthew 26:26.) What does the breaking of bread mean? Why do these disciples do this?

B What day is the first day of the week?

C The Christians seem to be gathering for the breaking of bread and a message from Paul on what day? What day was the Sabbath day? What day did Jesus rise from the dead (Matthew 28:1)?

Acts 20:8, 9

A Where is the young man Eutychus sitting? Is this a dangerous place?

B What seems to cause him to fall asleep?

C Imagine you are in this room. What would be your emotions when your friend Eutychus seemed to be dead?

Acts 20:10–12

A Does Paul get all upset?

B How badly hurt would someone be who fell from the third floor? What does Paul do when he sees what has happened?

C Paul's compassion for this young man is apparent, but what is Paul anxious to get back to doing? What time is it when these events are occurring? Paul's desire to give these people encouragement and truth is very evident here. Compare this with our Christian meetings.

Paul's journey is blessed by God, and those that have heard and accepted Jesus Christ as Saviour are also spreading the Good News. Paul knows that new Christians need God's Word and encouragement and he sets a good example for us.

Prayer

PAUL SAYS FAREWELL AT EPHESUS—ACTS 20:17–38

42

Prayer (Child)

Our Father in Heaven, thank You for this time You have given us to study the Bible. Guide our study, prepare us to hear, and to learn whatever You want to teach us, in Jesus' Name. *Amen.*

Scripture Reading (Head of Household)

Others follow along in their own Bibles.

Questions (Head of Household asks or chooses another to ask.)

FOR CHILD
1 What was the name of this famous man who preached about the Kingdom of God?
2 Where was Paul going?

FOR TEEN-AGER
1 What work had Paul done in Ephesus?
2 Who did Paul warn to turn from their sins to God and believe in the Lord Jesus?
3 How were the elders acting when they said good-bye to Paul?

FOR ADULT
1 Why was Paul going to Jerusalem?
2 What advice did Paul give to the elders for their church? Why?
3 Was life easy for Paul when he lived in Ephesus?

FOR ALL
Is there something in this passage that you can apply in your own life?

Prayer (Mother)

Thank You, Father, for this time of studying the Bible together. May Your Holy Spirit apply what we have learned in our lives, in Jesus' Name. *Amen.*

ACTS 21:1–16

43

Prayer

Begin with a prayer that the Holy Spirit open up the Scripture and discussion.

Read Scripture

To be read in the Living Bible or Living New Testament (if at all possible).

Questions

1 What was to happen to Paul according to the prophecy that was given? (*See* verse 11.)
2 What was Paul's response?
3 Why do you think he didn't agree not to go to Jerusalem? (Philippians 4:13 LB gives us a hint: ". . . for I can do everything God asks me to with the help of Christ who gives me the strength and power.")
4 Let's stop to put ourselves in Paul's place for a minute. What would be your first reaction, knowing what awaited you in Jerusalem? Discuss.
5 Even if he were to be thrown in prison or even be killed, in whom was he trusting?
6 Can you think of a time in your own life when something difficult or even frightening has happened to you? Discuss.
7 If the same thing were to happen to you now, knowing what you now know about Jesus, would you react in the same way?
8 If Paul trusted God so much that he could rest without fear in his big problem, couldn't we trust God with our everyday problems?

(Ever notice that no problem ever seems too big until it happens to you?)

Prayer Thought

Let's leave any problem we might have with God right now knowing that ". . . all that happens to us is working for our good if we love God and are fitting into his plans" (Romans 8:28 LB). Let us also ask Him for the faith to let go of our problems and then accept the peace that is ours as we do.

PAUL'S REPORT—ACTS 21:17–26

44

Prayer (Teen-ager)

Dear God, guide us as we study these words from the Bible. May our study be pleasing to You. Teach us by Your Holy Spirit to understand this passage, in the Name of Jesus Christ. *Amen.*

Introduction

Paul had been warned repeatedly not to go to Jerusalem because many of his followers feared for his safety. He knew by the Holy Spirit that "imprisonment and afflictions" awaited him (Acts 20:22, 23).

Read Scripture

The Revised Standard Version is used in this study.

Questions

1 Acts 21:17 How was Paul received by the brethren?
2 What did Paul relate to James and the elders?
3 Acts 21:20–22 What seemed to be their main concern about Paul's ministry and message?
4 Acts 21:20 Were they pleased to hear about Paul's ministry to the Gentiles?
5 What was Paul urged to do in order to placate the Jewish believers in Christ? We can learn about the vow in Numbers 6:13–21. Essentially, this vow was no longer necessary for a believer in Christ. Christ paid the penalty for our sins on the cross. His death was the supreme and final sacrifice needed for anyone who wanted his sins forgiven. The Jewish believers simply did not clearly understand Paul's message.
6 Do you understand what Paul's message was to the Gentiles? What are the key points?
7 How does one become a child of God with a zeal to witness? When we discuss our beliefs, we often clarify our thoughts and come to a better understanding of our own faith.

Food for Thought

1 Why do you think that Paul agreed to take the vow with the men? 1 Corinthians 9:20–22 certainly reveals Paul's thinking in this matter.
2 Paul's desire to become all things to all men in order to save some is very commendable. Have you tried to be all

things to all people in order to witness for Christ? Recall some of the things you have done.

Prayer (Mother)

Our heavenly Father, thank You for all that we have read and learned during this study. Thank You for spreading the Gospel through Paul and for Your love for all of us, in Jesus' Name. *Amen.*

PAUL ARRESTED IN JERUSALEM—ACTS 21:27–40

45

Prayer

Introduction

The "seven days" referred to in this opening verse is in reference to the Nazarite vow that Paul and four other men were fulfilling.

In the previous study, we noted that Paul knew that "imprisonment and afflictions" awaited him (Acts 20:22, 23).

Read Scripture

Questions

1 Acts 21:27–32 What reaction did Paul's presence in Jerusalem have on the crowds?
2 Why were the people so angry?
3 In the previous study, we learned that Paul agreed to take the Nazarite vow in order to placate the crowds and even convert some of them by becoming all things to all men. Did Paul's actions seem to have the desired effect?
4 Acts 21:33 How was Paul rescued from the mob?
5 Acts 21:33 In addition to being arrested, what did the tribune have done to Paul? In Acts 21:10, 11, Agabus, a prophet, foretold this incident.
6 Acts 21:31, 36 What had the mob hoped to do with Paul?
7 Where else in our studies of Scripture have we seen the very words of "Away with him" in connection with mob action? Christ, in John 19:15, heard the words "Away with him, away with him" from the mob before He was crucified.
8 Acts 21:39 What was the favor that Paul asked of the tribune?
9 In what language did Paul address the people?

Food for Thought

In our previous study, we discussed a facet of being all things to all men. How far can we carry this idea before our own witness has dwindled and maybe disappears? Think of examples in your own life.

Prayer

AN ANGRY MOB ATTACKS PAUL—ACTS 21:27; 22:1

46

Prayer (Father)

Our Father in heaven, help us to understand this part of the Bible. Teach us as we listen and read and think, through Jesus Christ. *Amen.*

Read Scripture (Teen-ager)

Others follow in your own Bible.

Questions (Father)

FOR CHILD
1 Whom did the angry Jews attack?
2 Where was Paul?

FOR TEEN-AGER
1 What did the angry crowd accuse Paul of doing?
2 How did the angry mob treat Paul physically?
3 What part do the Roman soldiers play in this violent attack on Paul?

FOR ADULT
1 How did the riot start?
2 For what reason was Paul arrested?
3 Why did the Roman commander give Paul permission to address the crowd?

FOR ALL
1 If you were near that mob which attacked Paul, how would you behave?
2 How does Jesus teach us to treat each other? Consider Ephesians 4:31, 32.

Prayer (Mother)

Father, we thank You for this real story, for the hardships Paul went through for the sake of Christ. Help us to live as You want us to live, in Jesus' Name. *Amen.*

PAUL SPEAKS TO THE ANGRY CROWD—ACTS 22:1–21

47

Prayer (Mother)

Almighty God, we seek to know more about You and Your will for our lives as we study Acts. Guide us as we study the Bible together, through Jesus Christ. *Amen.*

Introduction (Father)

Picture the scene: Moments before, Paul had been physically attacked by an angry mob which accused him of teaching against the Law of Moses and defiling the temple. They dragged him from the temple and tried to kill him. Just then Roman soldiers came and arrested Paul, probably saving his life. Paul wanted to speak to the people. The Roman commander gave his permission and, after the crowd quieted down, Paul spoke.

Read Scripture (Father)

Questions (Father)

FOR CHILD
1 Who is the person speaking?
2 Whose voice did Paul hear speaking to him on the road to Damascus?

FOR TEEN-AGER
1 What language did Paul use to speak to the crowd and why?
2 How would you describe Paul's encounter with Jesus on the road to Damascus?
3 In Paul's past, what had he done to Christians such as Stephen?

FOR ADULT
1 Why does Paul refer to his training as a Jew?
2 What message from God did Ananias give to Paul?

FOR ALL
1 What happened to Paul's eyesight? How did he get it back?
2 What did the Lord tell Paul to do?

Prayer (Child)

Thank You, Father, for all that we have read in these verses from the Bible. Help us to be brave Christians like Paul, in Jesus' Name. *Amen.*

ACTS 22:22–29

48

Prayer

Begin with a prayer that the Holy Spirit open up the Scripture and discussion.

Read Scripture

To be read in the Living Bible or Living New Testament (if at all possible).

Questions

1 In these verses, we get a picture of how a crowd can turn into an angry mob set off by even just one word. What was the word that made them so furious? (*See* Acts 22:21. For background, if necessary, *see also* Acts 21:26–29.)

2 We live in an age when there are many demonstrations and crowds that come together for different purposes. Some of them are good purposes. How do we learn from these verses that we must be careful to think for ourselves and not just follow the crowd?

3 Have you ever seen, personally or on television, or heard of a crowd that turned violent? Discuss.

4 Can you think of another time in the New Testament when a crowd turned against a completely innocent man? (*See* Matthew 27:15–26 to refresh your memory, if necessary.)

5 Jesus had the power to perform miracles. Why do you think He gave the crowd what they wanted and allowed Himself to be crucified? (*See* Mark 10:45. Notice that it says that He "gave." No one took Jesus' life from Him; He gave it willingly for us.) What difference does that make to you?

Prayer Thoughts

Realizing His great love for us, let's ask Him now to make us more obedient to Him, and even in a crowd, that we might still hear His voice.

PAUL BEFORE THE SANHEDRIN—ACTS 22:29; 23:11

(The Revised Standard Version is used in this study.)

49

Prayer

Introduction

In spite of Paul's marvelous defense, the crowd still wanted to do away with him. Paul was going to be scourged until they realized that he was a Roman citizen. Evidently it was unlawful for a Roman citizen to be treated in such a manner.

Read Scripture

Questions

1 Acts 22:30 How did the tribune attempt to find the real reason for the Jews' accusing Paul?

2 Acts 23:2 What was the high priest's reaction to Paul's opening statement before the council?
3 Acts 23:3 In anger and humiliation, how did Paul respond? (Jewish Law presumed a man's innocence until his guilt was proven.) Once Paul realized the identity of the man to whom he spoke, he showed the righteousness of his character and apologized. "You shall not revile God, nor curse a ruler of your people" (Exodus 22:28). Paul knew the Scriptures well.
4 Acts 23:6–8 How do the Sadducees and the Pharisees differ? Paul was humiliated or interrupted every time he tried to appeal to this council.
5 Another great clamor arose. What does the tribune decide to do with Paul? During this whole day, the tribune seems to be Paul's only friend.
6 Did the tribune ever find the real reason for the Jews' accusing Paul?
7 Acts 23:11 How did the Lord encourage Paul that night?

Food for Thought

Try to imagine how Paul felt after verse 10 of Acts 23. What a day he had! He came to Jerusalem to relate the success of his ministry to the Gentiles and possibly to win converts among his Jewish kinsmen. He had a great desire to go to Rome. The future of his ministry must have seemed bleak at this point. There he was in prison, dejected, disappointed, lonely, and a total failure. Have you ever reached such a low point in your life with some of Paul's probable feelings? How did you crawl out of that awful pit of despair? The Lord knew Paul's feelings that night. He had very similar experiences and verse 23:11 tells us that He "stood by" Paul. Paul must have been greatly encouraged. It is good for us to remember 1 Peter 5:7. The J. B. Phillips translation of the Bible states it so well: "You can throw the whole weight of your anxieties upon him, for you are his personal concern."

Prayer

(Reference: *The New Bible Commentary: Revised,* edited by Guthrie, D.; Motyer, J. A.; Stibbs, A. M.; Wiseman, D. J., p. 1004.)

THE JEWS PLOT TO KILL PAUL—ACTS 23:11–35

50

Prayer (Teen-ager)

Our Father, help us understand what You are saying to us as we study this part of the Bible. May Your will be done in our lives, in Jesus' Name. *Amen.*

Introduction (Father)

When Paul returned to Jerusalem to worship and bring gifts and report to the church elders after his third missionary journey, he was attacked by an angry mob of Jewish believers who threatened to kill him. Paul was saved by Roman soldiers who arrested him. He was permitted to defend himself before his own people, first the crowd, then the Jewish high priests and council. It was an opportunity for him to speak about Christ.

Read Scripture (Teen-ager)

Questions (Father)

FOR CHILD
1 Who stood by Paul at night while he was in the prison and told him to have courage?
2 Who finds out about the plot and tells Paul?

FOR TEEN-AGER
1 How many were in this plot to kill Paul? (What about the council and elders?)
2 How did God use Paul's nephew to help Paul?
3 What actions of Claudius Lysias made escape possible for Paul?

FOR ADULT
1 How do you think Paul felt when he was in prison before the Lord spoke to him and after the Lord spoke to him?
2 Why did the Roman commander send Paul to Governor Felix?

FOR ALL
1 What meaning does this passage have for you?
2 Read verse 11 again and remember it during the rest of Acts.

Prayer (Mother)

Heavenly Father, stand by us and help us to have courage in our times of trouble, in Christ's Name. *Amen.*

ACTS 24:1–9

51

Prayer

Begin with a prayer that the Holy Spirit open up the Scripture and discussion.

Read Scripture

To be read in the Living Bible or Living New Testament (if at all possible).

Questions

From verse 5 on, we find the Jewish leaders and their lawyer bringing charges against Paul.

1 What did they accuse him of?

2 Were the things they accused him of true? (*See* Acts 24:11–14.)

3 Paul wasn't the only one in the New Testament who was arrested on false charges. Do you remember when Jesus was arrested in the Garden of Gethsemane? (*See* Mark 14:53–56.)

4 Has anyone ever told a lie about you or anyone close to you?

5 How did you feel? Discuss.

6 When someone does speak falsely about us, what is the first thing we usually want to do? Discuss.

What did Jesus do when He was lied about, beaten, and finally hung on a cross? (*See* Luke 23:34.)

7 Jesus says in Matthew 5:44: "Love your enemies! Pray for those who persecute you!" and in Matthew 6:15, He tells us that we must forgive those who sin against us. Knowing this and knowing that we will never feel like loving and forgiving after we've been hurt by them, what must we do?

Does Jesus say we must feel like loving and forgiving, or does He just command us to do it?

Prayer Thoughts

Let's ask Him to fill us with love for others—even those who have wronged us in some way. If we have never forgiven them, let's forgive now, remembering that He is able to change our hearts and give us love, even for those we find hard to love.

ACTS 24:10–27

52

Prayer

Begin with a prayer that the Holy Spirit open up the Scripture and discussion.

Introduction

In the preceding verses, the High Priest, some of the Jewish elders, and their lawyer tried to bring false evidence against Paul.

Read Scripture

To be read in the Living Bible or Living New Testament (if at all possible).

Questions

1 What *did* Paul confess to in verses 14 and 15?
2 According to verse 16, because of what he believed, what did he try always to do?
3 How can *we* keep a clear conscience before God? How about before men? Discuss.
4 In verse 25, what was the reaction of Felix to what Paul told him? Why would he be terrified?
5 Once we know Jesus as our Lord and Saviour, should we have any fear about future judgment? Why?
6 If Felix only would have given Jesus first place in his life, he wouldn't have had to *fear* judgment, but from verses 26 and 27 we get two clues as to what was more important to him. What are they?
7 Does Jesus Christ have *first* place in your life? Why can't we allow anything or anyone else to become more important than He is? Do you remember the First Commandment? (*See* Exodus 20:2, 3.)

Prayer Thoughts

Let's take this time to examine ourselves to make sure nothing has become more important than Jesus in our lives, and if anything has, to confess it.

Let's thank Him now for what He has done for us on the cross so that we don't have to fear judgment.

PAUL APPEALS TO THE EMPEROR—ACTS 25:1–32

53

Prayer (Father)

Our Father in heaven, give us wisdom to hear what Your message is for us as we study this passage of Scripture. Guide us as we study, may it be pleasing to You, in Jesus' Name. *Amen.*

Introduction (Father)

Escorted safely from Jerusalem to Caesarea by Roman soldiers and horsemen, Paul was put in prison in Herod's palace. The Jewish high priest, some elders, and a lawyer followed him to Caesarea and accused him before Governor Felix. Paul denied all charges and told them of his belief in the Law, the prophets, and of his hope in God and life after death. For two years, Paul was held prisoner by Felix. Felix often called Paul in to talk and Paul talked to him about faith in Jesus Christ. But when Paul spoke about the coming Judgment Day, it frightened Felix, and he would send Paul away. Then Festus became the new governor and the Jewish leaders again accused Paul.

Scripture

Father chooses family members to read the parts of Governor Festus, Paul, King Agrippa. Others follow in own Bibles.

Questions (Father)

FOR CHILD
1 Had Paul done something wrong to the Jews?
2 What dead man did Paul say was alive?

FOR TEEN-AGER
1 Why did Festus ask Paul if he wanted to be tried in Jerusalem?
2 To whom did Paul appeal? (It was the right of every Roman citizen to appeal his case to the emperor.)
3 What important people came to welcome Festus?

FOR ADULTS
1 Why do you think Paul appealed to the highest Roman authority, the emperor?
2 What was the nature of the charges made against Paul as explained by Festus to the king?

FOR ALL
Can you apply something in this passage in your own life?

Prayer

Thank You, Father, for allowing us to learn about these events in Paul's life. May we see the Holy Spirit's work in his life. Help us to be patient and strong, too, in Jesus' Name. *Amen.*

KING AGRIPPA AND BERNICE HEAR PAUL'S DEFENSE—ACTS 26:1–27:1

54

Prayer (Teen-ager)

Almighty God, open our eyes to see, and our ears to hear, and our minds to understand Your truths as we study this part of the Bible, in Jesus' Name. *Amen.*

Introduction (Father)

Festus asked King Agrippa for his advice. The place for the meeting of Paul and the king was an audience hall. The Bible tells us that King Agrippa and Bernice came with much ceremony and honor (*see* Acts 25:23). The military chiefs and leading men of the city also attended, and Festus was host to this glamorous occasion. Listen to Paul speak!

Scripture

Father chooses family members to read the parts of Agrippa, Paul, and Festus.

Questions (Father)

FOR CHILD
1 What people came to this meeting?

FOR TEEN-AGER
1 What do Paul and Agrippa have in common and why?
2 What things about his life as a Pharisee does Paul tell Agrippa?
3 What did Jesus tell Paul that he was to tell others? How could they have their sins forgiven?

FOR ADULTS
1 What does Paul think Agrippa knows and believes?
2 What was Paul's prayer for all the people there? (Father asks someone to read verse 29 aloud.)

FOR ALL
1 What did Festus think Paul had become?
2 What comments are made by the king and the others after they had left the meeting?

3 How would you defend your faith in Jesus Christ?

Prayer (Mother)

Heavenly Father, thank You for telling us about Paul and for his witness for Jesus Christ, in His Name. *Amen.*

PAUL'S VOYAGE TO ROME—ACTS 27:1–12

55

Prayer (Father)

Guide us, Father, as we study this part of the Bible. Prepare us for the study, teach us to apply what we learn, in Jesus' Name. *Amen.*

Introduction (Father)

With Julius, a Roman centurion, in charge, Paul and some other prisoners boarded a ship at Adramyttium. The date of the departure is estimated as A.D. 60. Their destination was Rome, Italy. Paul wanted to go, Christ had told him to go, and his appeal to the Emperor to face him in Rome had been granted.

Read Scripture (Teen-ager)

Others may follow in their own Bibles.

Questions (Father)

1 To what country were they sailing?
2 Who was Julius? Was he kind to Paul?
3 What two friends sailed with Paul? (Aristarchus is also mentioned in Acts 19 and was probably a convert of Paul's.)
4 In Myra, they changed ships from a smaller vessel to the Alexandrian cargo ship. Did they have smooth sailing to safe harbors? Why not?
5 What advice did Paul give those in charge of the ship?
6 Why didn't they follow Paul's advice?

Suggestions

Pictures of a Roman centurion, ancient ships, and maps showing the areas of this voyage can be used during the three studies of Paul's voyage to Rome. Younger children may want to draw their own pictures of the ship.

Prayer (Mother)

Thank You God for this opportunity You have given us to read and study the Bible together, in Jesus' Name. *Amen.*

PAUL'S VOYAGE TO ROME—ACTS 27:13–38 (Continued)

56

Prayer (Mother)

Dear Father guide our family study of Paul's trip. Help us to understand the meaning of this passage of the Bible. May our eyes, ears, and lives be open to Your teaching, in Jesus' Name. *Amen.*

Introduction (Father)

Here are some interesting facts about the ship to keep in mind while picturing Paul and the rest on that storm-tossed sea.

It was made of wooden planks and probably about 180 feet long and 45 feet in breadth. On board was a cargo of wheat and 276 people. There was a foresail which could be raised or lowered, a foremast, mainsail, and mainmast. The sails were square and fastened to very large yards. According to custom, two eyes were painted or carved one on each side of the stern. On either side of the prow was painted or carved the ship's sign or name. An upward curving post was at the stern, and possibly the bow, the stern post ending in the head of a waterfowl. The deck was protected by a rail. There were anchors fore and aft much like modern anchors but without the flukes. The ship was steered by rudders which were flat planks or oars projecting through portholes on each side of the ship near the stern. Cables or chains called "helps" were on board to prevent leaking or foundering in a severe storm. In use, they were placed around the ship at right angles to its length and tightened. In a fair wind, the ship sailed at about seven knots. If the ship carried charts or instruments, they were imperfect and there was no compass. There were many ships trafficking the Mediterranean Sea in the first century. Besides storms and winds, there were dangerous coasts and sandbars to try to avoid.

Read Scripture (Father or volunteer)

Acts 27:13–38

Questions (Father)

1 What kind of weather did the ship encounter as it sailed along the coast of Crete?
2 What measures did the crew take to save the ship during the storm?
3 When did they give up hope of being saved?
4 Who appeared to Paul?

5 What did Paul tell the people that the angel said?
6 How did the sailors try to escape?
7 What did Paul beg the men to do?
8 How did Paul give them courage?

Prayer (Child)

Almighty God, Creator of the sea and wind, thank You for this time to study Your Word. Help us to be brave and strong, trusting in You, through Jesus Christ. *Amen.*

PAUL'S VOYAGE TO ROME—ACTS 27:39–28:15

57

Prayer (Mother)

Our Father in heaven, give us wisdom in understanding this part of Acts. Guide our family study. May it honor You, through Jesus Christ. *Amen.*

Introduction (Father)

Caught in a violent storm at sea for many days, the sailors did everything humanly possible to save the ship and their lives. They had given up all hopes when an angel of God appeared to Paul telling him that he must go before the Emperor and that everyone sailing with him would be saved. Paul told the people about this and urged them to eat. They ate and "took courage." Then came daylight and the shipwreck.

Read Scripture (Father)

Questions (Father)

1 How did the sailors try to get to the shore?
2 What happened to the ship?
3 How did Julius save Paul's life?
4 How did everyone get to the shore?
5 Whom did they meet on the island of Malta?
6 What special thing did God do for Paul when the snake bit him?
7 What did God do for the sick people on the island?
8 How long did the travelers stay on Malta?
9 What did Paul do when he got to Rome and saw his fellow Christians?
10 Who was taking care of Paul throughout the voyage?

(NOTE: It is estimated that the voyage took six months, ending in Rome about March first. Trace this trip on the map.)

Discuss

What does Paul's voyage to Rome mean to me? Further Bible reading: Psalms 107:23–32

Suggested Hymns

"Sing Praise to God Who Reigns Above," all verses; "For All the Saints From Their Labors Rest," all verses.

Prayer (Father)

God bless our family. Help us to seek and obey Your will for our lives through our Lord and Saviour Jesus Christ. *Amen.*

PAUL ENROUTE TO ROME—ACTS 28:1–16

(The Revised Standard Version is used in this study.)

58

Prayer

Introduction

Paul, a prisoner, is on his way to Rome. The ship he was on was wrecked, but Paul and the entire crew escaped safely to the island of Malta.

Read Scripture

1 Acts 28:2 How did the natives of Malta show kindness to Paul and the ship's crew?

2 What happened to Paul while he was helping with the fire? Was he hurt?

3 What was the reaction of the natives to this incident with the viper?

4 Acts 28:7 Who was Publius? How did he treat the shipwreck victims?

5 Acts 28:8, 9 How did Paul minister to the people of the island?

6 Acts 28:11 When did Paul leave Malta to continue his journey?

7 Acts 28:15 How do you know that the brethren in Rome were pleased to see Paul? What a glorious day it must have been for Paul. He had been looking forward to this occasion for a long time.

8 Acts 28:15 What was Paul's reaction to have finally come to Rome?

9 Acts 28:16 Since Paul was a prisoner, was he taken immediately to prison?

Food for Thought

Think about these verses on another level for a moment. Paul had a great desire to go to Rome, and he knew it was God's will for him (Acts 23:11 and 27:24). However, he almost seemed hindered in being able to reach Rome. He was in danger not only from the shipwreck, but also from the viper once he was safe on land. Can you see the hand of God on Paul? In spite of all the difficulties, everything seemed to work in his favor. Could the incident with the viper have caused the natives of Malta to be more willing to listen to him?

If we in our lives find our plans going amiss, or that our situation in life has taken a new and unexpected turn, could that be the hand of God in our lives? Can you think of times in your life when this may have been so?

Paul was in Rome as a prisoner. Do you think that his ministry was very much hindered by his imprisonment?

Prayer

PAUL IN ROME—ACTS 28:16–31

(The Revised Standard Version is used in this study.)

59

Prayer

Introduction

As a prisoner, Paul was permitted to live in his own house or apartment with the soldier that guarded him.

Read Scripture

Questions

1 Acts 28:17 Who did Paul call together?
2 For what reason did he want to speak with these Jewish leaders?
3 Acts 28:20 According to Paul, why was he a prisoner?
4 Acts 28:21 Had these Jews in Rome heard anything against Paul personally?
5 Acts 28:22 About what were they curious to hear?
6 To what sect were they referring?
7 Acts 28:23 What was Paul's message to the great numbers of people who came to his lodging?
8 Acts 28:24 How did the people react to Paul's message?
9 Paul recalled a quotation from Isaiah 6:9, 10 that seemed to apply to these people. What is the essence of that quotation (Acts 28:26, 27)?
10 Acts 28:28 This verse is a quotation from Psalms 67:2. In addition to the Jews, to whom is the message of salvation sent?
11 Acts 28:30 How long did Paul live in Rome preaching and teaching about Christ in an open and unhindered manner?

Food for Thought

1 Paul was a prisoner in Rome. His chains did not permit him to go to the synagogue and speak to the Jews he so much wanted to reach. Such a situation could have been a real handicap, but not for Paul. He preached and taught unhindered about Christ, while he was guarded and in chains! Think about your own situation and how you can be a witness for Christ.

2 Why do you think the Book of Acts ends the way it does, with an unfinished feeling to it? Enough is recorded for us to know how Christ's Church began. The growth of the church has continued to this day through the body of believers, and will continue until Christ returns.

Prayer

Be thankful for the Book of Acts and its messages to us.

DRAMA: PAUL AND SILAS—ACTS 16:16–34

Paul was told in a vision to go to Macedonia to preach the Good News. There, one of the first converts was a woman named Lydia, then her entire household. Paul and Silas stayed at her house and conducted prayer meetings beside the river. On their way to one of these meetings, they met a demon-possessed girl.

(Name various members of the family to play these roles while Father reads verses 16–34.)

Characters

Demon-possessed girl	Mob
Paul	Judges
Silas	Jailer

Girl's masters

(With such a large cast, some family members will have to play more than one part!)

OPEN-BOOK QUIZ—ACTS 10

To understand better how Peter felt about being in a Gentile's house, you have to understand the Laws about forbidden foods as set down in Leviticus. Read Leviticus 11 and make a list of twenty forbidden foods.

Read Acts 10:36–43 and fill in the blanks. (Use The Living Bible.)

1 Jesus was anointed with the H______ S______.
2 He went around doing g______.
3 He h______ everywhere.
4 He was m______ on a cross.
5 God raised Him on the third day, and He was seen alive by chosen witnesses!
6 He sent Peter and others to p______ the G______ N______ because Jesus is the J______ of all.
7 Everyone who b______ in Him will have his sins ______.

TRUE OR FALSE

a Cornelius, as a Gentile, was sincere, but not in the right religion.

b Cornelius had access to God through Jesus Christ just as Peter did.

c Cornelius would make it on his own because he was a moral, praying, giving man.

Divide Acts 10 into suggested titles for the following verses. (We'll give you a suggestion for the first one.)

Verses 1–8 Cornelius and the Angel
Verses 9–23 ____________________
Verses 24–33 ____________________
Verses 34–43 ____________________
Verses 44–48 ____________________

Studies in Ephesians

This is one of Paul's so-called prison letters, written around A.D. 62. It was probably a general letter sent to a group of churches in Asia Minor because the words "at Ephesus" (1:1) are not found in the oldest manuscripts. (You can get a "feel" of the background of this Epistle by reading Acts 18:18 through 20:1, 17–38 as well as Revelation 2:1–7. Paul spent three years in Ephesus, a busy commercial center and the site of the great temple of Diana, one of the wonders of the ancient world.)

Unlike Paul's other letters, it does not deal with specific problems within a particular church as do, for example, his Epistles to the Corinthians. It was a circular or general letter. Although considered by some the most impersonal of Paul's Epistles, it was very personal to those who received it. And even today, those who read it carefully will find it subjective. Those who study Ephesians over and over declare that they constantly get new insights into the wealth that the Christian has in Jesus Christ. Some stress the unity of the church (Jews and Gentiles, one in Christ). Others emphasize the fact that our salvation is a free gift (2:8, 9). Some particularly appreciate its emphasis on our relationships not only with Jesus Christ, but through Him to our husbands, wives, parents, children—in fact all with whom we come in contact. (It is interesting to note, too, that 75 of the 155 verses in Ephesians are also found in Colossians.) Chapters 1–3 are doctrinal, telling us of our spiritual possessions. Chapters 4–6 are practical—urging us to live up to our spiritual possessions.

Only six chapters in length, this is possibly one of the most frequently quoted of all Paul's letters. It will be interesting to see in your own family what the various members consider most important in Paul's letter to the Ephesians. (Because different authors have emphasized diverse aspects within the same chapters, for some passages there are two lessons covering the material, one marked *A* for "alternate." For a deeper understanding, you may want to do both lessons.)

EPHESIANS 1:1–7

1

Prayer

Begin with a prayer that the Holy Spirit open up the Scripture and discussion.

Read Scripture

Ephesians 1:1–6 (To be read from the Living Bible or Living New Testament, if possible.)

Questions

1 Who makes it possible for us to be adopted into God's family?
2 Why, do you think, would someone want to adopt someone else?
3 What does that tell us about how God feels about us?
4 What did Jesus have to give up so that we might be adopted?
5 Do you think He did it willingly? What does the Scripture say?

Ephesians 1:7

6 After we've confessed to God when we've done wrong and are really sorry, should we still feel guilty about the sin? (*See* Romans 3:22–24.)
7 Have you ever felt guilty? Discuss. Can you think of a specific time?
8 Did you ever find it hard to believe that God could forgive you?
9 Have someone put verse 7 in his own words. If verse 7 says that God forgives all our sins because of what Jesus has done for us, then how do you think God must feel when we don't accept His forgiveness?

Prayer suggestion

Remembering God's tremendous *love* for us (John 3:16)—we should take this time to confess to God if we have wronged anyone or to ask forgiveness for any sin that has never been confessed. Then, pray that we receive right now the forgiveness that is ours in Jesus Christ. (*See* 1 John 1:9.)

EPHESIANS 1:1–16

1A

Prayer

As we highlight the Book of Ephesians together, we will concentrate first on chapters 1 and 2 which deal with the believer's position in grace.

Introduction

In the very first verse, Paul begins by greeting the saints at Ephesus as loyal (or faithful) which is a welcome change from the Corinthians and Galatians who were in need of admonishment. Having reached this point, they are now ready to go on to further teaching.

Read Scripture

To begin, we will be discussing verses 3–14. Read these verses out loud or to yourselves, whichever suits you best.

Questions

1 On the basis of verses 4, 5, what is our relationship with God intended to be and through whom is this relationship acquired?
2 In God's plan, what is His ultimate purpose? (*See* verse 10.)
3 Read verse 7 chapter 1. What is the purpose of the shedding of blood? Is the shedding of blood essential to God's plan of salvation? Why? (*See* 1 John 1:7.)
4 There are nine promises or blessings in these verses (3–14). Can you find any or all of them?
5 What are the conditions for these blessings? (*See* John 3:16; 3:13.)
6 What, then, is our inheritance through Jesus Christ?

Prayer

Now is a good time for the family to consider the above and then bring together your needs and praises to the Lord for giving you the family you have.

(Recommended reading for this lesson is the booklet by E. W. Kenyon entitled "The Blood Covenant." It is published by Kenyon's Gospel Publishing Society, P.O. Box 33067, Seattle, Washington 98133.)

EPHESIANS 1:17–23

2

Prayer

Read Scripture

Questions

1 In chapter 1:17–19, what are some of the requests Paul asks of God for the Ephesians? Since they were already sons of God through Christ (*see* John 1:12), does this prayer request imply that they had not yet received all their earthly inheritance (or the fullness of God's blessings)? How does this apply to the believer today?

2 What do verses 20–23 tell us of Jesus Christ's position and authority? (*See* Matthew 28:18.) What does this mean to the believer in Christ (v. 19)? (*See also* John 14:12–15.)

3 Read verses 1–10, chapter 2. Compare man's old nature in verses 1–3 with that of the new man in verses 4–10. (*See* 2 Corinthians 5:17.) What changes take place? To whom was the old man obedient (verse 2)?

4 Paul says in verse 5 and in verse 8 that it is "by grace you have been saved" (RSV). What is God's grace? (You may want to look up *grace* in the dictionary.) The Living Bible gives a clear translation of this verse also.

5 After reading verses 8 and 9, can you explain what salvation is? Is it deserved or can it be earned?

6 Although we can never be put right with God by doing "good works," what place do they have in the Christian life?

Conclusion

The balance of this chapter deals with the reconciliation of Jews and Gentiles now being united in One Spirit, and that through Jesus now both have access to the Father (verse 18).

Verse 13 confirms "The Believer's Position Through Grace" in Ephesians 1:2.

To close you might want to sing together the hymn "Amazing Grace." The words seem to sum up what we have been discussing.

Amazing grace! How sweet the sound—
That saved a wretch like me!
I once was lost but now am found,
Was blind but now I see.

Prayer

EPHESIANS 2:1–10

3

Prayer

Introduction

Because way back in Genesis, man sinned against God, and God cannot look upon sin, Jesus came to earth to take away our sin. We now are able to talk to God in prayer and know that we belong to Him. Christ has restored our fellowship with God.

Read Scripture

Questions

1 Turn to Ephesians 2 and read verses 1–3.
  a What five things did we do before Christ saved us?
2 Now read verses 4–6.
  a What do these verses say about the kind of person God is?
  b What three things did God do for us through His Son, Jesus?
  c What did we do to deserve His kindness?
3 Read verses 7–10.
  a Why did God do all these things for us (v. 7)?
  b Can we in any way earn our salvation? What does verse 8 say about this?
  c What does God expect of us after we have accepted His gift of salvation?

You might enjoy singing the following chorus together.

Thank you Lord for saving my soul;
Thank you Lord for making me whole;
Thank you Lord for giving to me
Thy great salvation so rich and free.

Personal Sharing Time

Has each of us in this family accepted Jesus, God's wonderful gift, as our own personal Saviour? How can each of us who have accepted Him live closer to Him and do more for Him?

Prayer

Thank God for His wonderful Son, Jesus. Ask Him to help us to live and work faithfully for Him.

EPHESIANS 2:1–13

3A

Prayer

Begin with a prayer that the Holy Spirit will open up the Scripture and discussion.

(To be read in parts from The Living Bible, if possible)

Read

Ephesians 2:1–3

Questions

1 What do we learn about *us* and what we're really like from the first three verses?

Ephesians 2:4–9

2 What do we learn about God and what He is really like from these verses?

3 Verse 8 uses the word *saved.* Can you think of a time when one person might have to be "saved" by another person? Discuss.

4 If you were drowning and someone saved your life, how would you feel toward that person?

5 How do verses 8 and 9 show us that we need Jesus to save us from the way we are and that we can never earn salvation by being good enough? (Romans 3:21–23 LB tells us: "But now God has shown us a different way to heaven—not by 'being good enough' and trying to keep his laws, but by a new way. . . . Now God says he will . . . declare us 'not guilty'—if we trust Jesus Christ to take away our sins. And we all can be saved in this same way, by coming to Christ, no matter who we are or what we have been like. Yes, all have sinned; all fall short of God's glorious ideal.")

Ephesians 2:10–13

6 After we realize that we can never do enough good things to please God (verse 9) and that Jesus has already done it all for us (verse 13), what should we be doing with our lives (verse 10)?

7 In what way do you think God might want you to help someone else today? Discuss.

Closing Prayer

Remembering that He answers those who truly seek Him, pray that the Holy Spirit will open our eyes to "see" that Jesus is the Way. (*See* John 14:6.) That God will specifically show each one of us how we might be a blessing to someone else.

EPHESIANS 2:11–22

4

Prayer

Introduction

Paul was a Jew, but he felt called to preach to the Gentiles. Paul was very concerned that the Gentiles would realize that Christ died for all men everywhere, and that at the cross all men are equal. He has broken down all barriers and made us one with Him.

Read Scripture

Questions

1 Turn to Ephesians 2 and read verses 11–13.
  a What were the Gentiles like before Christ saved them?
  b What did the blood of Christ do for them?
2 Now read verses 14–18.
  a What two groups of people did Christ bring together through His death on the cross?
  b What did Christ give to both the Jews and the Gentiles?
3 Read verses 19–22.
  a What wonderful things happen to us when we become Christians?
  b What is the Christian together with Christ and other believers like?

Personal Sharing Time

Have you ever felt that you were better than someone else in school? sports? looks? your job? Were you ever unkind to someone for this reason? Did you ever feel that someone was better than you for these same reasons or others? How does today's lesson cause us to look at others as our equals?

Prayer

Thank God for the peace we have through His Son, Jesus, that we who believe are all members of God's family.

EPHESIANS 3:1–7

5

Prayer

Introduction

Paul feels it is necessary to explain to his readers about his call to preach the Gospel of Christ to the Gentiles. It was unheard of for a Jew like Paul to believe so strongly in the need for the Gentiles to share in the plan of salvation.

Read Scripture

Questions

1 Open your Bibles to Ephesians 3 and read verses 1–4.
   a Why was Paul a prisoner?
   b How did Paul feel about his call to preach to the Gentiles?
   c What is the "mystery of Christ" that Paul talks about in verse 4? (The answer is in verse 6.)

2 Now read verses 5–7.
   a What three blessings do the Gentiles share with the Jews (v. 6)?
   b What did God give Paul to use in telling others about Himself?

Personal Sharing Time

Did you ever feel that you wanted to help another person even though no one else shared your concern? Did you ever want to tell others about Jesus even though you were the only one doing so? Paul didn't worry about what others thought of him. He only wanted to please the Lord.

Prayer

Ask God to fill each heart with His power and the desire to tell others about Him.

EPHESIANS 3:8–13

6

Prayer

Introduction

Paul, overjoyed with the knowledge that he was the special person chosen to take the Gospel of Christ to the Gentiles, explains to them the wonderful riches that God has in store for them if they believe in Him. He tells them that he doesn't mind suffering so that they may know that salvation is for everyone.

Read Scripture

Questions

1 Turn to Ephesians 3 and read verses 8–10.
   a How does Paul describe himself?
   b What special blessing was given to Paul?
   c What was God's purpose in sending Paul to the Gentiles (v. 10)?

2 Now read verses 11–13.
   a Compare verse 11 with Ephesians 1:4. What do these say about God's plan for us?
   b What blessings are ours in verse 12?
   c What was Paul's attitude toward his suffering?

Personal Sharing Time

Have you ever suffered in any way (been embarrassed, missed a favorite function, given up some material possession) for the sake of another person coming to know the Lord?

Prayer

Thank the Lord that we have the same privilege as Paul of sharing Him with those around us, and ask Him to make us willing, unafraid witnesses for Him.

EPHESIANS 3:14–21

7

Prayer

Introduction

Paul, knowing that the Gentiles sometimes became discouraged and lacked faith, prayed this prayer to God that He, God, might, with His unlimited resources, fill them with His tremendous spiritual blessings.

Read Scripture

Questions

1 Turn to Ephesians and read chapter 3 verses 14–16.
   a In what position does Paul pray?
   b How does Paul describe God in these verses?
   c How does God give to His children?
   d What does Paul ask God for in verse 16?

2 Now read verses 17–19.
   a What four other blessings does Paul ask God for?

3 Read verses 20, 21.
   a How much can God do for us?
   b How is He able to do this?

Personal Sharing Time

What does it mean to you to have ". . . the mighty inner strengthening of his Holy Spirit" (v. 16 LB)? Discuss what it means to have ". . . your roots go down deep into the soil of God's marvelous love" (v. 17 LB).

Prayer

Quietly bow your head and, with Mother or Dad leading, pray the prayer that Paul prayed in verses 16b through 19 asking God as His dear children for these same spiritual blessings for your own heart.

EPHESIANS 4:1–13

8

Prayer

Pray that God will make His Word plain to each member of your family.

Introduction

Ephesians 1–3 describes the blessings given to believers in Christ.

In chapter 4, Paul begins to tell us how believers should behave. To help us to act in the right ways, Christ has given gifts to His Church. Paul quotes from Psalms 68:18 to remind us of a custom in biblical times: When the winning army returned home, its leader brought gifts to his people. Christ was the victor over Satan when He rose from the dead. Now He is able to give gifts to His people. These gifts are to help us to become the kind of people that God has planned for us to be.

Read Scripture

Questions

CHILDREN
1 What does Paul call himself (v. 1)?
2 Believers in Christ are called the "body of ______" (v. 12).
3 About whom should we be learning more (v. 13)?

TEENS
1 What four qualities of Christian living are mentioned in verse 2?
2 What is the kind of unity to which Paul refers in verse 3?

3 What are some gifts to the church (v. 11)?
4 Who should be the standard when we measure our spiritual lives (v. 13)?

ADULTS
1 What seven aspects of unity does Paul mention (v. 5, 6)?
2 How many believers receive gifts according to Christ's grace (v. 7)?
3 Why are gifted men given to the church (v. 12)?
4 What is the goal of our Christian walk (v. 13)?

What About Me?

Discuss the qualities of lowliness, meekness, patience, and forbearance. Have I shown these qualities in my relationships with others today?

What have I done to make peace today in my home? in my classroom? in my office? in church?

What is my gift from God for service for Him? Am I using it? If you do not know your gift (ability), pray that God will show you.

Springboard (optional)

Discuss the concept of gifts from God to be used in His service. Help your children to discover their gifts. Encourage them to develop their natural talents, and ask God to use them.

Make a further study of the topic of spiritual gifts in Scripture. (*See* Romans 11:29, 12:6; 1 Corinthians 7:7, 12; 1 Timothy 4:14; 2 Timothy 1:6; 1 Peter 4:10.)

Song

Sing "They'll Know We Are Christians by Our Love" (page 11, *A New Now*, Youth Folk Hymnal).

Prayer

EPHESIANS 4:14–24

9

Prayer

Pray for each member of your family to learn to do his part in the Church.

Introduction

If we believe in Christ as our Saviour, we are a part of His body, the Church. If we don't do our part, the whole body suffers. Paul tells us in this passage some of the things God wants us to do. Then Christ's body, the Church, can grow properly. The New

English Bible translates verse 16, ". . . the whole frame grows through the due activity of each part. . . ."

Read Scripture

Questions

CHILDREN
1 What are we told to speak (v. 15)?
2 In what ways are we to "grow up" in Christ (v. 15)?
3 Who is the head of the Church (v. 15)?
4 Who is our "new nature" to be like (v. 24 RSV)?

TEENS
1 How do the Gentiles live (v. 17)? What do you think this means?
2 Where is the truth found (v. 21)?
3 What are we to "put off" and "put on" (vs. 22–24)?
4 What are the characteristics of the "new man" (v. 24)?

ADULTS
1 What characteristic of children does Paul tell us to avoid (v. 14)?
2 How is the truth to be spoken? What is the result (v. 15)?
3 Why are the Gentiles alienated from God (v. 18)? Who are the "Gentiles" today?
4 What part of us is to be renewed (v. 23)?

What About Me?

What does it mean to "grow up" in Christ? Babies are not born full grown. Neither do believers in Christ begin as grown-up Christians. Help your children to see the areas where God wants to help them grow spiritually. What areas in your spiritual life are still "growing up"?

How do I obey the command, ". . . be renewed in the spirit of your mind" (Ephesians 4:23)? How should this affect the books I read, or the TV programs or movies I see? How should this affect my thoughts?

Springboard (optional)

Learn the chorus "Things Are Different Now," #732, *Living Hymns.*

The following passages are translations of Ephesians 4:17, telling how the "Gentiles" live: "in the vanity of their mind" (KJV); "in the futility of their minds" (RSV); "blindfold in a world of illusion" (PHILLIPS); "with their good-for-nothing notions . . . their wits are beclouded" (Ephesians 4:18 NEB).

Discuss how a person would act who lived in these ways.

Prayer

Ask God to show you things in your life that may need "renewing."

EPHESIANS 4:25–5:6

10

Prayer

Before reading and discussing this passage, ask God to show each of you the actions in your lives which are not Christlike.

Introduction

Little children learn by copying their parents. As they grow, they begin to resemble their parents in the way they walk and talk, and sometimes even in their appearances. Paul tells us to copy God in this same way. God showed us how to act when He became man. This Man, Christ, is to be our example. But God gives us more than an example to follow. He gives us the Holy Spirit who lives in each believer. The Holy Spirit guides us and gives us power to live like Christ.

Read Scripture

Questions

CHILDREN
1 What kinds of words should Christians speak (4:29)?
2 How should we act toward one another? Why (4:32)?
3 How did Christ show His love for us (5:2)?

TEENS
1 Why should we tell the truth (4:25)?
2 What is one reason for working (4:28)?
3 Why does God punish people (5:6)?
4 What specific characteristic of Christ are we told to copy (5:2)?

ADULTS
1 What does it mean to "let not the sun go down upon your wrath" (4:26)?
2 What seal or assurance of redemption has God given to the believer (4:30)?
3 Describe the kind of conversation that should characterize a Christian (4:29 and 5:3, 4).
4 What negative qualities should the Christian not exhibit (4:31 and 5:5)?

What About Me?

Is my life worldly or Christlike? If someone was describing my life, what would he say?

How do I handle my anger? Do I hold grudges, or try to make peace right away?

If someone had recorded my conversation today, would I be ashamed to hear it played back?

Springboard (optional)

Discover as a family the joy of doing loving deeds for each other. Encourage one another to do a kind deed or say a kind word to each family member once a day. Then have a report time in the evening with each member reporting the "love gifts" he received that day.

Discuss ways in which Christians may grieve the Holy Spirit.

Prayer

Ask God to make each family member sensitive to the guidance of the Holy Spirit in his talk and action.

EPHESIANS 4:17–32

10A

Prayer

Begin with a prayer that the Holy Spirit open up the Scripture and discussion.

Read Scripture

(To be read in The Living Bible or Living New Testament, if possible.)

Questions

1 The Scripture talks about a person who "closes his heart" to God. How can someone do this? Discuss. What does the Bible say happens to a person whose heart has been closed?

2 From verses 22–24, we learn that we have been given a new nature because of what Jesus Christ has done for us. What does the Scripture say we must do with our old nature? Discuss.

3 If we really put Jesus Christ first in our lives, why can we no longer lie, hold a grudge against someone, steal, use bad language, or be bad tempered? What about when everyone else does these things?

4 The Bible doesn't say we won't be tempted to do some of these things (1 Corinthians 10:13 LB), but, when we *give in* to the temptation, who are we allowing to have a place in our lives?

5 What two things do we learn about the Holy Spirit from verse 30?

6 Read verse 32 again. Why should we be kind and forgiving toward others? Is there anyone in your life that you have not forgiven for some wrong that he has done to you? (*See also* Matthew 6:12, 14, 15 LB for what Jesus has to say about forgiveness.)

Suggestions (optional)

Claim verse 32 as a family verse and try to have each one memorize it. It helps to remember it in those "tough moments." Refer to Matthew 6:14, 15 and see the results of an unforgiving heart.

Prayer

Remembering God's mighty power at work within us (Ephesians 3:20), pray that He will keep us from giving in to temptation, and that we might be loving and kind to each other.

EPHESIANS 5:1–20

11

Prayer

Dear Lord, through this lesson please help each of us to learn more about walking in the light of Your Son, Jesus Christ. *Amen.*

Read Scripture

Questions

When a little boy walks just like his father, we say he imitates his father. Who does our Heavenly Father want us to imitate?

If we imitate God, what are some of the things we will do?

What are some of the things we will not do if we are trying to be like Jesus?

Will those who enjoy doing the things they know God doesn't like have an inheritance in His Kingdom?

If we are truly Christians in our hearts and know Jesus Christ as our Saviour and Lord, God wants us to walk as children of light. What does this mean we should try to do?

What things should children of light avoid?

Why is it important to be thankful to the Lord for everything in our lives?

Does this mean we should be thankful for the things we don't like, too? Why?

The end of these verses suggests that we should speak to each other in psalms, hymns, and spiritual songs. Select one or two things you would like to sing as a family and sing them now. (*See* Song Index for suggestions or your favorite hymnal.)

Discuss (optional)

What influence do our friends have on us? Discuss. (1 Corinthians 15:33 RSV warns us: "Bad company ruins good morals.")

Prayer

Remembering that "God is love" (1 John 4:16), pray that His love might flow through us to others.

EPHESIANS 5:7–21

11A

Prayer

Pray that the Holy Spirit will show where sin is present in your lives.

Introduction

Paul continues describing the qualities of the believer's life. The life of the unbeliever is darkness, but the life of the believer is light. He should no longer act like the ones in darkness. The light of Christ shows us the actions which are pleasing to God.

Read Scripture

Questions

CHILDREN
1 Who are we to try to please (v. 10)?
2 Who gives us light (v. 14)?
3 What does verse 19 tell us to do?
4 For what things should we be thankful (v. 20)?

TEENS
1 What are the characteristics of "children of light" (vs. 8–9)?
2 How does a wise man live (vs. 15, 16)?
3 What does this passage say about drinking wine (v. 18)?
4 What does this passage say about hymn singing (v. 19)?

ADULTS
1 What should our position be with regard to the sinful activities of unbelievers (v. 11)?
2 What does the light do (v. 13)?
3 What contrasts are presented in this passage?
4 What attitude should we exhibit toward other believers? Why (v. 21)?

What About Me?

How did my life measure up today? Were my actions good, righteous, and true?

Do I make good use of my time? What are my priorities—what do I do first?

Am I submissive to others, or do I always defend my rights?

Springboard

Spend time singing some hymns such as "I Would Be True."

Discuss the contrast between being drunk with wine, and being filled with the Spirit. How does a person act in each case?

Prayer

Ask God to empower your family to obey the light Christ has given to them.

EPHESIANS 5:21–33; 6:1–4

12

Prayer

Begin with a prayer that the Holy Spirit open up the Scripture and discussion.

Read Scripture

Ephesians 5:21–33 (To be read in the Living Bible or Living New Testament.)

(The dictionary defines *submit* as follows: to refer to the decision or judgment of another. The Amplified New Testament describes submission as being subject—adapting yourself to another.)

Questions

1 What is the relationship of a husband and wife compared to in verse 23? Discuss.

2 Who has God placed as "head" of the home? How does this differ from what we see, hear, and read today? What about Women's Lib?

3 If we obey the Scripture, how should a husband treat his wife? How should a wife act toward her husband?

4 If we obey the Bible in our relationships with one another, who then is honored?

Read

Ephesians 6:1–4

5 According to these verses, why should a child obey his or her parents?

6 The commandment says to "honor" your father and mother. Discuss what "honoring them" means to you. If you were to really honor and obey them, would there be a change in the way you behave?

When we pray according to His will, God answers prayer.

Prayer suggestion for today

PARENTS That we allow the Lord to work within each of us to restore the proper order in our relationships. That we don't irritate and provoke our children by scolding and nagging, but that we might bring them up in the loving discipline of the Lord (verse 4).

CHILDREN That we may honor and obey our parents.

EPHESIANS 5:22–33

13

Prayer

Pray that your family may truly be a *Christian* family, where Jesus Christ is glorified.

Introduction

Paul has been speaking to all believers. Now he has some instructions for specific people. God's love is not for mankind as a group, but as individuals. He cares about our daily activities as mother, father, or child. But, more importantly, He has a plan for our way of living as mother, father, or child.

Read Scripture

Questions

CHILDREN
1 Who is the head of the family (v. 23)?
2 Who is the head of the Church (v. 23)?
3 How should a husband act toward his wife (v. 28)?

TEENS
1 What change takes place in family relationships when a person marries (v. 31)?
2 Is it important for a believer to marry only another believer? What is the measuring stick of a wife's submission (v. 22)? . . . of a husband's love (v. 25)?
3 What has Christ done for the Church? What are His future plans for the Church (vs. 26, 27)?

ADULTS
1 What should the wife's attitude be towards her husband (vs. 22, 33)?
2 In what areas should the wife be subject to her husband (v. 24)?
3 What should characterize the husband's life with his wife (vs. 23, 25, 28, 31, 33)?

What About Me?

WIVES Do I give in to my husband in everything? Should I?

HUSBANDS Do I love my wife in the same way Christ loved the Church? Do I sacrifice myself for her?

TEENS Can a woman who is not submissive to the Lord become submissive to her husband? Can a man who does not know Christ's love, adequately love his wife? What qualities am I looking for in a wife or husband?

Springboard

Discuss some of the present-day views of marriage. Compare them to God's plan for a Christian marriage.

Prayer

Pray for God's strength to be a family that is pleasing to God in its relationships to each other.

EPHESIANS 5:21–33

13A

Prayer

Read Scripture

Questions

What would happen if an orchestra tried to play music without any leader?

In order for orchestra music to sound beautiful, the orchestra must have a leader to tell each musician when to play. A family is like an orchestra. In order for everyone to work and play well together in a family, there must be a leader. Who has God made the leader of the family?

What kind of a leader does God want the husband to be?

What is the goal of the husband's leadership?

God gives us a picture in Ephesians of how the relationship between a husband and wife should be. What example does God use to show us?

How does God want the wife to respond to her husband's leadership?

If the wife obeys as unto the Lord in the way God asks her to, how does this work for her good?

Do you think the kind of marriage we read about in Ephesians is possible if the husband and wife are not Christians?

Prayer

Dear Lord, teach us through Your Holy Spirit, we pray to follow Your plan for leadership in our home. Help us to obey You so that our home will be a place of love and blessing. *Amen.*

EPHESIANS 6:1–4

14

Prayer

Read Scripture

Questions

Just as God has a plan for mothers and fathers in the family, He has a plan for children, too. What does God tell children they should do?

What would happen if children didn't obey their parents?

Why should children obey their parents?

When the Bible says, "Honor your father and mother" (6:2 RSV) what does it mean?

What is God's promise to those who do honor their parents?

Fathers have many responsibilities as the leaders of their families. God helps fathers through His Word to know how to handle these responsibilities. Do you know some things from other parts of the Bible that fathers are to do?

What does Ephesians tell fathers *not* to do?

How can fathers bring up their children in the discipline and instruction of the Lord?

If you have time, discuss with your children how understanding God's order for family life makes it easier to see why families have a leader and why children should be obedient followers. Discuss ways in which your family could make some changes to follow God's plan better.

Prayer

Pray for your family to be obedient to all God teaches about being members of a family.

EPHESIANS 6:5–9

15

Prayer

Read Scripture

Questions

What is God's instruction to slaves?

How does God describe the way they should obey their masters?

Who should the slave be seeking to please by doing his best work?

What is the servant's reward from the Lord?

Do these verses apply only to slaves?

What is the real point of this section of Scripture?

What is God's direction to the master?

Does God look at the master in a different light than the slave?

Is this passage of Scripture an endorsement of slavery, or is it talking about something deeper than our position in life?

Learning to please God rather than men is a very important lesson. After giving your family a moment to think about it, discuss ways that people today can please God rather than men, or, more specifically, ways they see that they themselves can change their attitudes to please God more.

Prayer

Dear Lord, we pray that You will work in our lives to make us more eager to please You in everything we do and say. Help us not to be motivated by what people will think, but by what You will think. *Amen.*

EPHESIANS 6:10–20

16

Prayer

Read Scripture

Questions

Can one of you tell us what armor was like and how it was used?

Why did knights need armor?

Why do we need armor?

What does this passage in Scripture say we are fighting against?

What help does God provide for us in the battle?

Reread verses 14–16 and point out the important parts of God's armor. Talk about what they mean.

In verse 18, what does the Apostle Paul tell us will be a great help?

Although the king provides armor for his knights, will it protect them if they do not put it on?

Discuss with your family ways to "put on the whole armour of God." Emphasize the part each believer must have in using what God has provided for his help and protection.

Prayer

Dear Father, thank You for the things You have provided to keep us safe and to help us. Help each one of us to realize that *we* have a responsibility to use what You have given to us. *Amen.*

EPHESIANS 5

16A

Prayer

The next two lessons will be highlighting chapters 5 and 6. They continue to deal with Christian living, particularly within the family.

Read

Ephesians 5

Questions

1 In 5:1 we are told, as God's children, to be imitators of our heavenly Father, as children often imitate their earthly father. What responsibility does this place on the head of the home?

2 (Read verses 3–14.) Who will not inherit the Kingdom of God? What should our relationship be to these people (verse 7)? (See note at the end of lesson.)

3 Who is the Light of the world? According to these verses, what should be the results in those who are walking in the light?

4 Why do you suppose children of disobedience (those who have allowed Satan to control them) would rather do their evil deeds in darkness and are afraid to be exposed to the light (*see* verses 12, 13)?

5 In verses 17–21, there are at least six commands to the believer. What are they? What do they mean to you?

6 Some commands of God are easier to understand than others, but being obedient always brings blessings. Verse 20 tells us to give thanks for everything (read 1 Thessalonians 5:18). If you have never been able to do it before, now might be the time to think about those things for which you have never been able to be thankful. Talk about them together and if possible agree to pray about one another's needs in this area. There is "power in praise." The Word of God tells us often to praise and thank God. Look up Romans 8:28 for the results of trusting God and thanking Him in all situations.

NOTE: God loves all men and it is His will that none should perish and that all should come to a personal relationship with Him. Though we are told not to associate with their wrong doings (verse 11), we are taught to love all men and to share the Good News of Jesus Christ with them.

Prayer

Being obedient to verse 19, close by making music in your hearts to the Lord. If you know it, sing the chorus of "In My Heart There Rings a Melody" or the "Doxology" which is full of praise to God.

EPHESIANS 5 AND 6 (Continued)

17

Prayer

Introduction

This last lesson deals specifically with the divine order that God has set forth for the home. If this is new to you, it may be difficult to understand and even perhaps to accept at first, but remember this is God's Word and His direction for us. This is for a purpose. If a home is in and remains in the order that God has set forth, then nothing can come against it. In these days, when families are falling apart all around us, it is very reassuring to know that, if we are obedient to His Word, our homes and families will remain intact. An example and reference here would be in Matthew 7:24–27 and Luke 6:47–49 which tells about the man who builds his house upon the solid rock (the Word of God) and all things came against it, but it could not fall, because it was founded upon the rock. At the end of the lesson, books will be recommended that might help to better understand these chapters.

Read

Ephesians 5:21–32 (The cross-reference to this section is 1 Peter 3:1–7.)

Questions

1 Are we to be submissive to other Christians even if they do not have particularly pleasing qualities or characteristics? Why (v. 21)?
2 According to these verses, what should the order of leadership be within the home?
3 What are a wife's responsibilities to her husband? Does her obedience carry through to things that a husband might ask

of his wife that are sinful or wrong? To whom is she responsible first? (*See* the First Commandment, Matthew 22:37.)

4 What responsibilities does a husband have to his wife? What kind of love is he to have for his wife? Why is it the husband who is commanded to exercise this sacrificial love? (NOTE: Loving your wife as you love yourself means wanting to treat her in the same way that you would want to be treated.)

5 How does Paul compare the husband and wife relationship with that of Christ and the Church? The Living Bible Ephesians 5:31, says, "A man must leave his father and mother when he marries, so that he can be perfectly joined to his wife, and the two shall be one." Can we conclude that this illustrates that nothing should come between or hinder or separate the two in the same way that nothing should come between our relationship with Jesus Christ (*see* verse 32)?

(Also read chapter 6 verses 1–4 RSV.)

6 What does "in the Lord" mean? What is the promise that accompanies this well-known commandment? List ways in which you can honor your parents.

7 The responsibility and warning is issued directly to the father in verse 4. Why? What happens to the child if this is not obeyed? (*See* Colossians 3:21.)

8 How can parents know the proper balance of discipline? (*See* Ephesians 5:1, 2 and James 1:5.)

Prayer

Now is a good time for the family to consider the above and then bring together your needs and praises to the Lord for giving you the family you have.

(Recommended reading: *The Christian Family* by Larry Christenson; *Do Yourself a Favor: Love Your Wife* by H. Page Williams.)

AUTHOR BIOGRAPHIES

Marjorie (Mrs. James) Bloom, three children, graduate Houghton (N.Y.) College, junior-high-school English teacher, Sunday-school and vacation-Bible school superintendent, program chairman cooperative nursery.

Barbara (Mrs. William) Cook, three children, graduate Northeastern Bible (N.J.) College, graduate (B.S.) Nyack (N.Y.) College, elementary teacher in Christian school, Director, Christian Education in her church.

Martha (Mrs. Frederick) Grosser, four grown children, B.S. Wheaton (Ill.) College, R.N. Presbyterian Hospital (Ill.), involved in neighborhood Bible study group and teaches Sunday school.

Marcia Anne (Mrs. Thom) Hopler, four children, B.A. Barrington (R.I.) College, R.N. Roger Williams General Hospital (R.I.), served as missionary nurse in Kenya, led Bible study groups in Africa and the U.S.

Roberta (Mrs. John) Lee, three children, graduate Green Mountain (Vt.) College, participant in local church choir and Pioneer Girls group, active in three Bible study groups, PTA board member.

Janice (Mrs. Robert) McCarthy, three children, attended modeling school, senior high youth sponsor, along with husband leads other couples in Bible studies, family involved in personal ministry to ex-convict and family.

Carolyn (Mrs. C. Theodore) Ogren, three children, attended Wheaton (Mass.) College, B.S. Iowa State University, choir, active in Bible study groups six years, lived overseas and in six states as wife of U.S. Army officer.

Dorothy (Mrs. John) Rasmussen, four children, graduate Prairie Bible (Canada) Institute, eighteen years missionary service in Nigeria, Costa Rica, U.S., church visitation group, teaches women's Sunday-school class.

Hilda (Mrs. Edward) Remmers, three children, R.N. Lutheran Deaconess Hospital (Minneapolis), B.S. in Nursing Columbia (N.Y.) University, church visitation group, studying Scripture since 1966, Sunday-school teacher.

Virginia (Mrs. Stephen) Sirinides, six children, attended Hunter (N.Y.) College, B.A. Wheaton (Ill.) College, Masters in Nursing Yale (Conn.) University, Bible study group, choir director, advisor Board of Education.

Patricia (Mrs. Bruce) Stark, two children, actively involved in Bible Club work with children, eight years in neighborhood Bible studies and women's Bible studies, "school of the Spirit" in private devotions.

Sandra (Mrs. William) Van Dyk, four adopted children (two from Ecuador), attended Drew (N.J.) University, taught college students and adults in Sunday school, founder, youth retreat center, Waterbrook, PTA treasurer.

Jean (Mrs. Robert) Winkler, five grown children, attended Kings (Del.) College and Nyack (N.Y.) College, Sunday-school superintendent, church choir, PTA, involved in Bible study groups for ten years.

Editor: Betsey (Mrs. John) Scanlan, five children, B.A. Bucknell (Pa.) University, free-lance writer, on board of religious education for church four years, six years as Associate Editor for Fleming H. Revell Company.

BIBLIOGRAPHY

Allen, Charles L. *The Miracle of Love.* Old Tappan, N.J.: Fleming H. Revell Company, 1972.

Barker, William P. *Everyone in the Bible.* Old Tappan, N.J.: Fleming H. Revell Company, 1966.

Benedict, Robert P. *Journey Away From God.* Old Tappan, N.J.: Fleming H. Revell Company, 1972.

Blaiklock, Walter M. *The Acts of the Apostles.* Grand Rapids: Wm. B. Eerdmans Publishing Company, 1959.

Bowman, Mary D. *Love, Honor and . . . ?* Old Tappan, N.J.: Fleming H. Revell Company, 1970.

Bryant, Anita. *Bless This House.* Old Tappan, N.J.: Fleming H. Revell Company, 1972.

Cambron, Mark G. *Bible Doctrines.* Grand Rapids: The Zondervan Corporation, 1954.

Children's Bible, The. Racine: Western Publishing Company, Inc., Golden Press.

Christenson, Larry. *The Christian Family.* Minneapolis: Bethany Fellowship, Inc., 1970.

Davis, John D. *A Dictionary of the Bible.* 4th rev. ed. Westwood, N.J.: Fleming H. Revell Company, 1924.

Dunnett, Walter M. *An Outline of New Testament Survey.* Chicago: Moody Press, 1960.

Eade, Alfred Thompson. *The New "Panorama" Bible Study Course No. 2: The Study of Angelology.* Westwood, N.J.: Fleming H. Revell Company, 1962.

Evans, Louis H. *Your Marriage—Duel or Duet?* Westwood, N.J.: Fleming H. Revell Company, 1962.

Gariepy, Henry. *Portraits of Christ.* Old Tappan, N.J.: Fleming H. Revell Company, 1974.

Guthrie, D.; Motyer, J. A.; Stubbs, A. M.; and Wiseman, J. D. *The New Bible Commentary.* Rev. ed. Grand Rapids: Wm. B. Eerdmans Publishing Company, 1970.

Halley, Henry H. *Pocket Bible Handbook.* Chicago: Henry H. Halley, 1948.

Hartley, Al. "My Brother's Keeper." *Spire Christian Comics.* Old Tappan, N.J.: Fleming H. Revell Company, 1974.

Henry, Matthew. *A Commentary on the Whole Bible.* Genesis to Deuteronomy, vol. 1. Old Tappan, N.J.: Fleming H. Revell Company.

———. *Understanding the Gospel of John.* Old Tappan, N.J.: Fleming H. Revell Company.

Hodgkin, A. M. *Christ in All the Scriptures.* 13th ed. Westwood, N.J.: Fleming H. Revell Company, 1907.

Kidner, F. Derek. *Genesis: Tyndale Old Testament Commentary.* Downers Grove, Ill.: Inter-Varsity Press, 1968.

Leavell, Landrum P. *Angels, Angels, Angels.* Nashville: Broadman Press, 1973.

Lindsey, Hal and Carlson, C. C. *Satan Is Alive and Well on Planet Earth.* Grand Rapids: The Zondervan Corporation, 1972.

Mackintosh, C. H. *Genesis to Deuteronomy: Notes on the Pentateuch.* Neptune, N.J.: Loizeaux Brothers, 1972.

Mears, Henrietta C. *What the Bible Is All About.* Glendale: Gospel Light Publications, Regal Books, 1966.

Morgan, G. Campbell. *The Gospel According to John.* Old Tappan, N.J.: Fleming H. Revell Company.

———. *The Acts of the Apostles.* Old Tappan, N.J.: Fleming H. Revell Company, 1924.

Morrison, A. Cressy. *Man Does Not Stand Alone.* Westwood, N.J.: Fleming H. Revell Company, 1944.

———. *Seven Reasons Why a Scientist Believes in God.* Old Tappan, N.J.: Fleming H. Revell Company, 1962.

Needham, Mrs. George C. *Angels and Demons.* Chicago: Moody Press

Newport, John. *Demons, Demons, Demons.* Nashville: Broadman Press, 1972

Phillips, J. B. *Your God Is Too Small.* 25th ed. New York: Macmillan Incorporated, 1969.

Schultz, Samuel J. *Old Testament Speaks.* New York: Harper & Row, Publishers, 1970.

Scroggie, W. Graham. *A Guide to the Gospels.* Old Tappan, N.J.: Fleming H. Revell Company, 1948.

Smith, Hannah Whitall. *The Christian's Secret of a Happy Life.* New York: Fleming H. Revell Company, 1883.

Smith, William. *Smith's Bible Dictionary.* Westwood, N.J.: Fleming H. Revell Company, Spire Books, 1967.

Strachen, Elizabeth W. *A Mother's Wages.* Chicago: Moody Press.

Sweeting, George. *And the Greatest of These.* Old Tappan, N.J.: Fleming H. Revell Company, 1968.

Tozer, A. W. *Knowledge of the Holy.* New York: Harper & Row, Publishers, 1961.

Unger, Merrill F. *Unger's Bible Handbook.* Chicago: Moody Press, 1966.

Westcott, B. F. *The Gospel According to St. John.* Grand Rapids: Wm. B. Eerdmans Publishing Company, 1958.

Williams, H. Page. *Do Yourself a Favor: Love Your Wife.* Plainfield, N.J.: Logos International, 1973.

INDEX OF SONGS AND THEIR SOURCES

The following have been suggested by the authors of this book. Some can be found in more than one hymnal as well as in sheet music, records, or tapes. Those indicated as being in public domain or "traditional" can be found in a wide variety of sources. If your family doesn't already have a favorite hymnal, you'll probably want to select one.

FATHER OF JESUS CHRIST, MY LORD 39
by Charles Wesley
(Cross-Reference: "Faith, Mighty Faith.")
Public Domain

FOR ALL THE SAINTS WHO FROM THEIR LABORS REST 210
by W. W. How
#602 *The Covenant Hymnal*
Covenant Press
3200 W. Foster Avenue
Chicago, Illinois 60625

GIVE ME THY HEART 94
by E. E. Hewitt
#366 *Great Hymns of the Faith*
The Zondervan Corporation
1415 Lake Drive S.E.
Grand Rapids, Michigan 49506

GO TO DARK GETHSEMANE 138
by James Montgomery
#119 *Great Hymns of the Faith*
The Zondervan Corporation
1415 Lake Drive S.E.
Grand Rapids, Michigan 49506

GREAT IS THY FAITHFULNESS 178
by Thomas O. Chisholm
#403 *Inspiring Hymns*
The Zondervan Corporation
1415 Lake Drive S.E.
Grand Rapids, Michigan 49506

HALLELUJAH! WHAT A SAVIOR 120, 139
by P. P. Bliss
#302 *Inspiring Hymns*
The Zondervan Corporation
1415 Lake Drive S.E.
Grand Rapids, Michigan 49506

HOW GREAT THOU ART 15, 54, 166
by Stuart K. Hine
(Copyright © held by Manna Music, Inc.)
Worship in Song—Nazarene Hymnal
Nazarene Publishing House
Box 527
Kansas City, Missouri 64141

I GAVE MY LIFE FOR THEE 142
by Frances R. Havergal
#375 *Great Hymns of the Faith*
The Zondervan Corporation
1415 Lake Drive S.E.
Grand Rapids, Michigan 49506

I HAVE DECIDED TO FOLLOW JESUS 172
#397 *Great Hymns of the Faith*
The Zondervan Corporation
1415 Lake Drive S.E.
Grand Rapids, Michigan 49506

SING PRAISE TO GOD WHO REIGNS ABOVE 210
by Johann J. Schutz
#1 *The Covenant Hymnal*
Covenant Press
3200 W. Foster Avenue
Chicago, Illinois 60625

THANK YOU, LORD, FOR SAVING MY SOUL 218
(Copyright held by Alfred B. Smith)
Sunday School Sings
Gospel Light Publications
110 West Broadway
Glendale, California 91204

THE GREAT PHYSICIAN NOW IS HERE 171
by William Hunter
#59 *Great Hymns of the Faith*
The Zondervan Corporation
1415 Lake Drive S.E.
Grand Rapids, Michigan 49506

THE LIGHT OF THE WORLD IS JESUS 119
by P. P. Bliss
#335 *Inspiring Hymns*
The Zondervan Corporation
1415 Lake Drive S.E.
Grand Rapids, Michigan 49506

THEY'LL KNOW WE ARE CHRISTIANS
BY OUR LOVE 224
#11 *A New Now,* Youth Folk Hymnal
Hope Publishing Company
Carol Stream, Illinois 60187

THINGS ARE DIFFERENT NOW 225
#732 *Living Hymns*
Encore Publications © 1972
Drawer A
Montrose, Pennsylvania 18801

'TIS MIDNIGHT; AND ON OLIVE'S BROW 138
by William Bingham Tappan
#411 *Inspiring Hymns*
The Zondervan Corporation
1415 Lake Drive S.E.
Grand Rapids, Michigan 49506

TO GOD BE THE GLORY 167, 192
by Fanny Crosby
#152 *Hymns of Praise Number Two*
Carol Stream, Illinois 60187

TURN YOUR EYES UPON JESUS 33
by Helen Lemmel
#220 *Worship and Service Hymnal*
The Zondervan Corporation
1415 Lake Drive S.E.
Grand Rapids, Michigan 49506

General Index